Voices for the Future

Liz Mohn, Wolfgang Schüssel

Voices for the Future

20 Years of the Trilogue Salzburg

| Verlag Bertelsmann**Stiftung**

Bibliographic information published by the Deutsche Nationalbibliothek

The Deutsche Nationalbibliothek lists this publication in the
Deutsche Nationalbibliografie; detailed bibliographic data
is available on the Internet at http://dnb.dnb.de.

© 2022 Verlag Bertelsmann Stiftung, Gütersloh
Responsible: Jörg Habich
Translation: Tim Schroder, Frankfurt am Main
Production editor: Christiane Raffel
Cover Design and Typesetting: Büro für Grafische Gestaltung –
Kerstin Schröder, Bielefeld
Printing: Hans Gieselmann Druck und Medienhaus GmbH & Co. KG,
Bielefeld
ISBN 978-3-86793-948-5 (print)
ISBN 978-3-86793-949-2 (e-book PDF)
ISBN 978-3-86793-950-8 (e-book EPUB)

www.bertelsmann-stiftung.org/publications

Content

The Trilogue Salzburg
2001–2021

Acknowledgements

For 20 years, the Trilogue Salzburg has been a source of knowledge and inspiration, thanks to the objective, open dialogue it facilitates among political, economic and cultural representatives from all over the world. Its goal has been to make the world a bit better, more peaceful and more humane. Many of the global challenges that concern us today were already being discussed at the Trilogue at a time when few decision makers had them on their agendas – something this publication impressively documents as it looks back over the event's 20-year history. We would like to thank those who have been part of the Trilogue Salzburg not only for their forward-looking contributions, but also for the intensive, trusting exchange that has given rise to such close ties between the participants.

Liz Mohn   Wolfgang Schüssel

Preface

Wolfgang Schüssel, Liz Mohn

The future will be challenging. Not only is that statement true today, during the Covid-19 pandemic, it was true 20 years ago as well. As preparations were being made for the first Trilogue Salzburg, which took place in August 2002, there was no shortage of events suggesting the future would be somewhat bleak, or at least promising to have an enormous impact on what was to come. As an aide to memory, here are a few notable happenings from back then: On September 11, 2001, a terrorist attack leveled the World Trade Center and killed thousands of people. Europe was taking on a new shape as Greece joined the eurozone in 2001, and 12 EU member states introduced the coins and banknotes of their common currency at the beginning of 2002. At the EU summit in Copenhagen in December 2002, the decision was made to welcome 10 new members. In a referendum in Switzerland in 2001, three-quarters of the population voted not to engage in negotiations to accede to the EU – and a few years later, comprehensive bilateral agreements were signed. In 2002, Switzerland became the 190th member of the United Nations. At the end of 2001, China joined the World Trade Organization (WTO).

In the first decade of the new century, there was a spirit of change and optimism in the air, and much was in flux, above all in Europe. We were all looking for ideas that could move us forward. Art in all its guises served as a source of inspiration, but how would it be possible to introduce and implement these ideas in the political and economic arenas? As German philosopher Moritz Carrière put it, "To shape the particular from the idea is the purview of art; to grasp

the idea from its various sides by thought, to shape the idea of the
state, of art, of humanity itself on the basis of the real and the given,
by virtue of foresighted imagination and conclusive reasoning, is
the purview of philosophy."

The Salzburg Festival was conceived during the First World War's
darkest hour; the first *Everyman* stage was carpentered from boards
used for a barrack that housed prisoners of war. Resistance and intrigues
notwithstanding, Max Reinhardt succeeded in establishing the summer festival in Salzburg. Reinhardt exemplified the concept of learning by doing, of renewal – even after horrendous catastrophes such as
the world war. His credo was, "When one senses that routine has
begun creeping in, that's always the time to try something new."

All of these considerations gave rise to the Trilogue Salzburg:
a gathering of leading individuals from the cultural, economic and
political spheres, from as many countries and global regions as
possible, who would meet unencumbered by the concerns of daily
life to discuss and reflect, inspired by the Salzburg Festival's mag-
nificent performances. The idea was to combine impulses from all
three areas – thus the name "Trilogue" – so that something new
could take shape.

The significance of art and culture was and is tangible at the
Trilogue Salzburg, as artists make meaningful contributions to
reconciliation, understanding and peace, not to mention innovation.
Art moves and rattles us – "ice picks against the frozen sea in us,"
as Franz Kafka put it. The Trilogue provides art – which must often
defend itself from being preempted or appropriated – with a platform
of equal standing. One unforgettable moment was the participation
of director Andrea Breth, who came to Salzburg with great skepticism,
but then enthusiastically embraced both the format and interdisci-
plinary thinking, enriching them with her comments. Wonderful
musicians like Thomas Hampson, Franz Welser-Möst, Clemens
Hellsberg, Valery Gergiev, exceptional directors like Jürgen Flimm,
brilliant authors like Marc Elsberg and screenwriter Joan Xu have
taken part in the Trilogue – which would have been impossible to
realize without the active participation of Helga Rabl-Stadler, president of the Salzburg Festival, who has never failed to provide the
event's attendees with a personal introduction to the performance
they are about to see.

The issues we have addressed in the Trilogue's 20-year history have never served to address the past, but have always looked to the future, true to Albert Einstein's motto, "I'm more interested in the future than in the past, because the future is where I intend to live." The scope of the discussions has been wide, depending on what the future seemed to be promising at any given point in time and what merited a closer look. Topics have ranged from the search for identity to the question of how high-quality, sustainable economic development can be achieved and competitiveness maintained, to the various facets of globalization, Asia's rise, successful neighborhood policy, and the difference between perception and reality.

The Trilogue Salzburg was never meant to be an art-for-art's-sake event. The intention has always been to serve as a generator of ideas and impetus – for business and politics in Germany and Austria, but above all in Europe. The city of Salzburg was never located on a silk road, but a salt road that provided prosperity early on. Undoubtedly the city's most famous artist, Wolfgang Amadeus Mozart, was born there and contributed to Salzburg's becoming a cultural center. Hardly any location in the heart of Europe is better suited for contemplation and entertaining new trains of thought. This vibrant heart – Central Europe, in fact – offers enormous potential and also serves as a bridge to the East and Far East. The Trilogue has reflected this as well.

A range of perspectives can be found at the Trilogue, not only because of the different professions present; regional differences also offer new vantage points. The contrast in the way Europe is seen internally and externally is particularly great: The image of decay, of disintegration is often conveyed – the EU as a sick man, as a sinking ship or estranged family, home to blockades, intrigues, petty fights. Naturally, no one can deny that problems and disputes exist. Yet the opposite is also true: The EU sets standards that are considered exemplary from the US to China. The EU assists and supports, creates security and stability through peace missions and responsibly allocated development aid. Since the fall of the Berlin Wall in 1989, €400 billion has been disbursed to the EU's new member states – a huge expression of solidarity and many times more than the US made available through its Marshall Plan after the Second World War. A gentle giant, the EU makes our planet more livable, sustainable, open and secure – even if it is not always aware of its considerable power.

In his essay *After Europe*, Bulgarian political scientist and Trilogue participant Ivan Krastev analyzes how democracy and globalization have changed: "What was until recently a competition between two distinctive forms of government – democracy and authoritarianism – has evolved in the wake of the global financial crisis into a competition between two different forms of the statement: 'There is no alternative politics.'" Krastev criticizes that even in democracies, policy decisions are increasingly presented as having no alternative – which, after all, contradicts the very nature of democracy. The Trilogue has always been a search for possible alternatives, for best practices, for new pathways – as the quintessence of every democracy, as nourishment for free, independent citizens.

Apropos freedom: It has undoubtedly suffered the most during the Covid-19 pandemic. Not only because of the clear restrictions on movement, the social distancing and lockdowns. The state's paternalism is evident far beyond its pandemic-management efforts. No European politician is promoting the EU these days as a force of openness, one that transcends borders even on the continent itself, or advocates in the wider world for liberalization, free trade and political progress. All of Europe is bunkering down and putting up barriers. The EU now seems to be, first and foremost, a defense mechanism and bulwark – against Chinese corporate acquisitions and American digital enterprises, against illegal migrants and against the threat of dumping from post-Brexit Britain. A Europe that curls itself up like a hedgehog and spreads it spines is not our idea of Europe. Anyone who fears freedom should consider the words of former US President Thomas Jefferson: "Timid men prefer the calm of despotism to the tempestuous sea of liberty."

Jean Monnet once said he would, in a second attempt, give the European project a cultural foundation. That is an interesting and at the same time disquieting thought. It is precisely its diversity that makes our European way of life unique. That is even truer for the global community. Perhaps cultural exchange, translation, communication, contact, jointly organized festivals – without hegemony or a mania for centralization – would allow peaceful coexistence to flourish among the world's peoples. That was ultimately what

Monnet was pursuing with the European idea: "We are not uniting states, we are bringing people closer together."

If, in the 20 years that the Trilogue Salzburg has been taking place, it has succeeded in bringing at least a few people closer together and igniting some new ideas, then they can be seen as wonderful injections of courage for the future – whatever it might bring.

TRILOGUE SALZBURG

ARTS-ECONOMICS-POLITICS

Courage in an Age Lacking Courage: An Appeal

Helga Rabl-Stadler
President of the Salzburg Festival

"Our Salzburg Festival House is meant to be a symbol. It is not the founding of a theater, not a project called to life by a few starry-eyed fantasists, and not the undertaking of a provincial town. It is a matter of European culture. And of eminent political, economic and social importance." Those were the self-assured, urgent and unmistakable words used by poet and Salzburg Festival founder, Hugo von Hofmannsthal, as he described the task Salzburg faced 100 years ago.

And in his 1917 memorandum, composed in the midst of "the ravages of this war," von Hofmannsthal's congenial partner, director Max Reinhardt, wrote of the "terrible reality of our days," of the "conflagration enveloping the world" that the Salzburg Festival could and should repudiate. Founding a festival was meant to be "one of the first works of peace." The festival owes its existence to this firm belief in the power of art and in Salzburg as a seat of power.

It seems entirely logical to me that the Trilogue was founded at the beginning of the new millennium in the "heart of the heart of Europe" (as Hofmannsthal defined my hometown). Above all, I would like to thank Liz Mohn in particular for mobilizing all of the Bertelsmann Stiftung's intellectual and organizational resources, and for continuing to make them available. I would like to thank Wolfgang Schüssel that the decision was made in favor of Salzburg. After all, this city is ideal for thinking about the world, for thinking anew and thinking ahead.

What Reinhardt postulated about the festival applies here, too, to some extent. He was convinced that the exceptional could only be achieved "at a remove from the everyday bustle of city life" and "far from the distractions of the metropolis." The gatherings at the Trilogue, which usually give rise to inspiring exchanges after just a few hours, show that he was right. And the evening visits to the festival have always been more than mere entertainment – if I may say so.

"Art is a language that uncovers the hidden, tears open the sealed, makes tangible what is innermost, one that warns, excites, unsettles, gladdens." That is what the great Austrian conductor Nikolaus Harnoncourt passionately proclaimed to the audience during his remarks as the Salzburg Festival celebrated its 75th anniversary. "A work of art that wants to inspire, to move, needs qualified rejection as much as it needs approval" and "the great artworks are masterpieces because they always have something to say to people – even if every generation sees something different." The title of his remarks was "What Is Truth? or Zeitgeist and Trends."

Especially today, policy makers from all parties are tempted to follow the zeitgeist, allowing them to celebrate quick successes online. To me, that makes art's contribution all the more important. No, artists are not smarter, they do not occupy the moral high ground. But in a time of hasty answers, they know how to ask questions that force – at best, inspire – the public to reflect.

Max Reinhardt, Hugo von Hofmannsthal and Richard Strauss were firmly convinced that antique mythology offered subtle possibilities for interpreting modern problems of both a personal and political nature. Von Hofmannsthal, Strauss's favorite librettist, put it thus: "For if this age of ours is anything, it is mythical – I know of no other expression for an existence which unfolds in the face of such vast horizons – for this being surrounded by millennia, for this influx of Orient and Occident into our self, for this immense inner breadth, these mad inner tensions, this being here and elsewhere, which is the mark of our life. It is impossible to catch all this in middle-class dialogues. Let us write mythological operas! Believe me, they are the truest of all forms."

Our operas *Salome* and, this year, *Elektra*, provide impressive, breathtaking proof of this thesis. The temporal distance enables us to clearly see, as with a magnifying glass, the eternally valid conflicts: war and peace, love and hatred, forgiveness and revenge.

And anyone looking for change architects could very well find them among our artists. Director Peter Sellars incorporated environmental issues into his productions long before Greta Thunberg took to the streets for the same cause – not bathetically, not using a sledgehammer, but with an artist's sensibility for the looming catastrophe.

The Trilogue gave representatives of art and culture an equal place at the table with captains of industry and government ministers, so they could negotiate the future – a position we had to struggle for in the quotidian political arena during the pandemic. Everything else seemed more important – the hospitality industry, retail, the agricultural lobby. Yet the longer the lockdown went on, the more people quoted Reinhardt: art not as mere decoration, but as nourishment. And suddenly, the Salzburg Festival was again being praised for being what it was originally created to be: a beacon in dark times.

In April 2020, however, sympathies were not on our side. At a time when practically all other festivals were being cancelled, one feuilleton writer for a German-language publication stooped to the scurrilous assertion that "the Salzburg Festival undoubtedly wanted to become the cultural world's Ischgl."

Should we have allowed the coronavirus to wrest control completely and let the long-planned 100th anniversary of the world's largest classical music festival simply go unobserved? Or was it more appropriate to carry out the event – while always giving the health of our artists, employees and audiences top priority, of course – so it could set an example of the power of art in a powerless time? No one could give us advice, there were no precedents to look to. The mood at the highest leadership levels was – and remains – marked by uncertainty, whether in business, politics or culture.

The lockdown imposed by governments was followed by an equally fatal lockdown in the brains, in the responses of those who should actually be leading, be thinking of alternatives. That the Metropolitan Opera closed its doors in March 2020 and announced it would reopen sometime in the autumn of 2021 after an incredible 18 months is not merely a loss for opera fans. It will be a blot on New York's reputation as a cultural metropolis for a long time to come. It discredits the value of art. Art and culture are nourishment. They are essential services.

The Salzburg Festival provides both meaning and employment – we were always aware of this dual responsibility when we took the risk of performing during the pandemic. It was a calculated risk, not a gamble. We acted in keeping with an idea advanced by Peter F. Drucker, the first management guru: "There is the risk you cannot afford to take, and there is the risk you cannot afford not to take." Had we cancelled, our lack of courage would have been a cause for shame in light of our founding fathers, who believed in the need for festivals in much more difficult times.

Last year's summer season was at times a veritable purgatory – even as the pandemic continues to cast its shadow over us this year as well. But by September we had near-heavenly results: a sold-out festival, a giant step forward in terms of digitalization, a thousand good ideas on how we can offer faster and even better service to our greatest asset, our loyal customers from 80 countries around the world.

I am certain that my appeal for courage in an age lacking courage will be well received, especially by Trilogue participants, and to that end I would like to cite Hugo von Hofmannsthal once more: "When the will alone bestirs itself, something has almost already been attained."

I very much hope that, in the coming decade, the Trilogue will continue to infect decision makers from around the world with the will to engage in discourse and debate.

Europe's Role in the World

The aftermath of the financial and debt crisis has not yet been overcome, the consequences of the Covid-19 pandemic cannot yet be foreseen, relations with neighboring countries have not been defined, the question of the extended workbench has not been answered, and the refugee issue has not been resolved. There are, moreover, self-inflicted shortcomings, since Europe's basic values are ignored when convenient, Brexit remains unsettling and lessons have yet to be learned from vaccination-distribution efforts. Not to mention the problems that ensue when populists call the entire notion of a unified Europe into question, or when expectations are raised and demands made from both within and without. Europe currently faces numerous challenges that are affecting the continent's very foundations and ability to coexist.

Europe has experienced – and survived – dramatic crises again and again. Not by merely putting up with everything, but by responding to and overcoming crises when they happen. One strength in this regard is Europe's diversity – and we Europeans should be proud of our manifold lifestyle, which many in the world admire and feel is worth emulating. Yet more and more people here have little appreciation for our own way of life. It's paradoxical: On the one hand, Europe and the European Union are, in this age of globalization, bigger, stronger and more influential than ever before. On the other, the continent has seldom seemed more hesitant and divided internally: Communal rules are broken, solidarity merits no more than a wan smile. Purported national interests are praised instead.

Yet what is this Europe? Which role are we talking about that Europe must, can or should assume in the world? Is it time to redefine the role of the "European house," and does it even need a new role in the world at all? Does a common understanding exist of these issues? Is a robust vision needed if Europe's role in the world is to be respecified?

The emergence of Europe as we know it

Geographically, Europe forms, together with Asia, the continent of Eurasia and is therefore "only" a subcontinent – the western fifth of the Eurasian land mass. Distinct boundaries, such as the North Atlantic and Mediterranean, do not exist to clearly differentiate

Europe's Borders

● EU member   ● EU accession candidate   ····· Europe's geographical border

Source: Authors' depiction

Europe from Asia, which is why cartographers and politicians have always been confronted with the question of which countries should be counted as part of the European continent. The vague border runs along the Ural Mountains and Ural River to the Caspian Sea, as well as to the Caucasus Mountains, Black Sea and Bosporus. This Europe comprises between 47 and 49 sovereign states lying wholly or partly within these borders.

Yet Europe has long been much more than just a geographic concept. Historically, it has been marked by the colonies that individual countries established during the age of imperialism, allowing them to generate wealth and exert political influence. Moreover, the onset of industrialization turned Europe and its nations into a global region of growth and prosperity. But the frequent assertion of national interests led to wars initiated by – and waged in – European countries. The return of troops from all parts of the world after the First World War allowed the Spanish flu to spread globally, causing further suffering. After several years of peace and reconstruction, fascism and the Second World War followed, which once again put a spotlight on the European continent as a central theater of war and led to widespread destruction of lives, property and natural resources.

After the Second World War, the Cold War – combined with the founding of a European Economic Community – divided the continent into Eastern and Western Europe. Correspondingly, common rules were established for a European Community predicated on solidarity, economic growth, democratic values and the hope for peace. With the reunification of Germany, the demise of the Warsaw Pact and the disintegration of the Soviet Union, fears faded that the Cold War might turn hot.

The vision of a united Europe

Europe, however, has long been much more than just a shared history – and its experiences and lessons from the past should be used to inform its future role. Although its different cultures and religions have led to conflict in the past – and in some cases continue to do so today – they can now, thanks to numerous shared values, coexist peacefully and enrich our European way of life. First and foremost, the inviolability of human dignity is seen as especially worthy of protection here, and is regarded as the cornerstone of all basic rights. Also fundamental for Europe's communal life is the freedom its citizens have to express their opinion, choose their religious affiliation and assemble without having to fear (government) persecution or exclusion. Representative democracy, the equality of all citizens, the rule of law and human rights are other values and goals that have been laid out by the European Union in the Treaty of Lisbon and the EU's Charter of Fundamental Rights.

Yet Europe means much more than a shared understanding of values. At the latest since Konrad Adenauer and Robert Schuman, it has been a political factor, behind which stand a political will and political force for shaping events. After all, throughout history European states have repeatedly formed alliances, such as the Congress of Vienna, the Council of Europe, the European Union and the Conference on Security and Co-operation in Europe (CSCE). These have served to achieve common objectives and prevent conflicts among states, thus improving lives on the continent, preserving peace and promoting prosperity.

To that extent, Europe is also an idea, a vision, a cohesiveness. And, no, this idea is not perfect and many things must be improved. Yet can the answer be to focus on going it alone and on the things that divide? How are peace, freedom and prosperity to be ensured if everyone in Europe proceeds down a different path once again? And how is a fractious Europe supposed to help shape the world we live in? Would such a Europe be taken seriously by the world's other powers? After all, this vision of a united Europe was and is the foundation for prosperity and growth.

One of Europe's milestones in the 21st century was the introduction of a common currency. It has facilitated trade within the eurozone and strengthened the pre-existing single market. Free trade agreements with nations and alliances around the world guarantee that, within the global economy, the union itself is now seen as important, instead of individual European states.

At the same time, digitalization is accelerating and easing international communication and global trade. The world is growing even closer together and the younger generation in particular enjoys a range of opportunities. For example, when young people seek

European Values

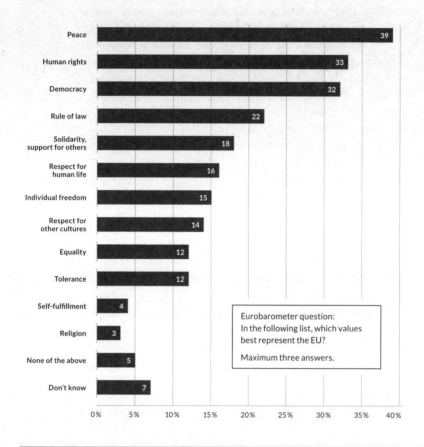

Peace — 39
Human rights — 33
Democracy — 32
Rule of law — 22
Solidarity, support for others — 18
Respect for human life — 16
Individual freedom — 15
Respect for other cultures — 14
Equality — 12
Tolerance — 12
Self-fulfillment — 4
Religion — 3
None of the above — 5
Don't know — 7

Eurobarometer question:
In the following list, which values best represent the EU?

Maximum three answers.

Source: European Commission. Eurobarometer 89: European Citizenship. 03/2018.

employment, they can choose a job not only in their home country, but also in numerous countries around the world. However, the negative effects that can result from a global economy of this sort were made apparent by the worldwide economic crisis and subsequent euro crisis. Both events not only devoured trillions in financial resources, they also weakened the trust and hope many young people have in the EU. The member states' high levels of debt reduced their room for maneuver in terms of policy responses, and made joint solutions necessary.

Yet Europe is much more than an economic power. It is the joint search for solutions to crises that affect all European states to varying degrees. Since the outbreak of civil war in Syria at the latest, the ongoing influx of refugees has repeatedly confronted the EU with challenges in terms of its migration and foreign policy. At the same time, it should not be forgotten that those of us living in the relatively prosperous countries north of the Mediterranean do not bear the main burdens that result from dislocation and displacement. Those fall instead on the countries bordering the crises, to which people first flee from war, persecution and devastation. Although the political divisions between Eastern and Western Europe seemed to have been overcome at the beginning of the century, the annexation of the Crimean Peninsula by Russia made a new EU security policy necessary. Additionally, a trend towards Euroskepticism became evident in the 2014 European elections, one that has been reinforced since then by increasing nationalism in more and more countries.

While many Europeans view democracy as the best political system for their country, they increasingly doubt how effective policy makers can be. The growing presence of populist parties in Europe's parliaments is also increasingly altering today's democracy. Many people now see this as a threat to liberal democracy, whose success very much depends on the courage to compromise. How can we strengthen cohesion in (European) society in the future, so we can continue to live and share the humane, democratic values we know? Not least, the UK's departure from the European Union raises the question of how Europe's role will evolve over time.

So we see that Europe plays a different role depending on the point of view, and that, given how it sees itself, it must fulfill not one, but numerous roles. Our job is to define and determine what

European Government Debt

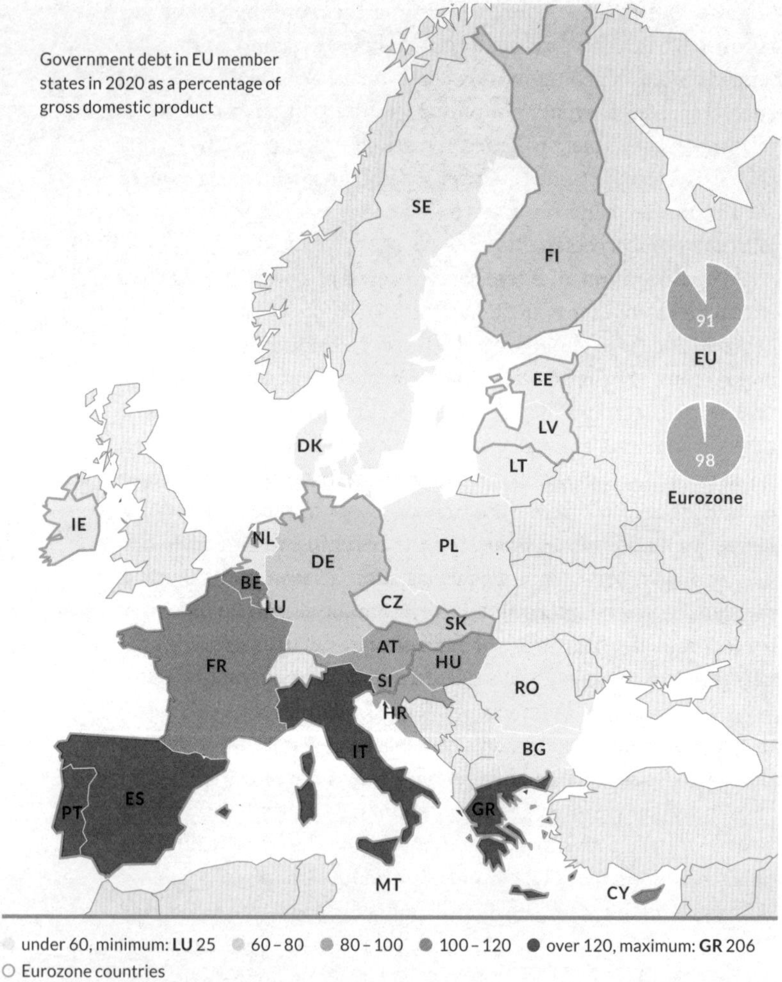

Government debt in EU member
states in 2020 as a percentage of
gross domestic product

91
EU

98
Eurozone

SE
FI
EE
LV
DK
LT
IE
NL
PL
DE
BE
LU
CZ
SK
AT
HU
FR
SI
RO
HR
IT
BG
PT
ES
GR
MT
CY

● under 60, minimum: **LU** 25 ● 60 – 80 ● 80 – 100 ● 100 – 120 ● over 120, maximum: **GR** 206
○ Eurozone countries

Source: Eurostat; authors' calculations

they are. Yet no continent can define its role independently of its neighbors and the global community of states, nor can it overcome all by itself the challenges it will face over time. No country can develop solutions on its own. We are witnessing the rise of many Asian nations, especially China. Many people in these countries are now better off. Yet can we join with them to find a new, a shared, a peaceful way to coexist – politically and economically? After all, we live neither in a European nor in an American, not even in an Asian century. We live in a global century.

Partnership with neighbors

For the first time, we are experiencing the dangers wrought by a global virus, including its impact on politics, business and society. Covid-19 knows no borders. Yet we are also experiencing cooperation in the fight against the virus – across borders, continents, religions, ideologies, world views. Shouldn't global threats connect us in the future instead of dividing us? We have yet to achieve global solidarity. Europe's future role, however, will depend on how it is defined in terms of its interactions with other world regions, and how Europe's relationship – or, more precisely, that of the European Union – is shaped vis-à-vis other regions.

This necessarily includes reflecting the status quo in the countries located directly next door. The European Neighbourhood Policy (ENP) focuses on providing the EU's immediate neighbors to the south and east with incentives to implement reforms in the areas of rule of law and democracy. At the same time, the countries themselves decide to what degree they will develop ties to the EU on this basis. Numerous individual measures have also been designed to promote relations: Programs for fostering regional cooperation among the partner countries themselves and with the EU include the Eastern Partnership (EaP), which was established in May 2009 under the Czech EU Council presidency; in addition, the Union for the Mediterranean (UfM), established in July 2008 under the French EU Council presidency, is meant to play a key role as a multilateral forum for political dialogue and regional cooperation. Here, the EU serves primarily as an economic partner and mediator for its near neighbors. When it comes to formulating its own objectives and interests vis-à-vis its neighbors, however, the EU is largely reticent. Yet the inherent danger in having multiple individual undertakings is that people lose sight of the big picture.

Thus, any future role must include less micromanagement and, in its place, multiple and more efficient key policy lines. Nonetheless, it will not be possible to overcome all the challenges at once. We must instead begin with the questions that matter now: How can we work together to protect our external borders? How can we work together to ensure peace beyond those borders? Shouldn't we develop a common security and defense strategy?

International touchpoints

The African continent is one of the most important foreign policy actors for Europe. The EU and the African Union have maintained close ties for years so they can collaborate to promote security, climate protection, investment and education. Key undertakings here include the Cotonou Agreement, as well as the Joint Africa-EU Strategy (JAES), which was adopted by European and African heads of state and government in Lisbon in 2007. With that, the EU took on the role of largest foreign investor. Since 60 percent of people in Africa are under the age of 25, one objective is to create jobs locally. Moreover, the EU supports African countries through numerous missions to train soldiers, police officers and judges, and it is fighting piracy off the Horn of Africa through the EU NAVFOR mission.

In the area of environmental protection as well, the EU and its member states contribute significant amounts to support biodiversity, environmental and species protection, and renewable energies. Since more than € 173 billion worth of goods were exported to African countries in the Mediterranean region in 2019 alone, efforts are being made to conclude a joint free trade agreement. The largest challenge is undoubtedly population growth. The fertility rate in Niger, for example, is the highest in the world and the average age of the country's population is just under 15 years.

Europe's role will therefore be shaped by its own sluggish demographic growth relative to a rapidly growing Africa, whose population will double by the end of this century. That could create pressure to migrate that lasts for decades, something which could not be managed with inadequate rules and institutions. We may assume that in the coming years and decades, more and more people will attempt to reach the longed-for destination of Europe by one means or another. That is why the European Union must consider creating a common border and migration policy. Europe will have to take a unified stance – and not by looking for someone to blame and pointing fingers at each other, but by developing joint solutions.

We must also define Europe's role within the interplay of trans-atlantic relations with the US and Canada. Although the same values of democracy, human rights and rule of law are shared by those on both sides of the Atlantic, and economic ties between the Old and the New Worlds are still close, the American continent has not proven immune to the populism, nationalism and protectionism that have been sprouting up around the globe. In recent years, what had been a secure flank in the "ring of fire" surrounding Europe since the Second World War has become less predictable. On the political level, relations have been strained by the US's decisions to withdraw from the Paris climate agreement and from the Iran nuclear deal.

On the economic level, the Trump administration was a completely different negotiating partner than the EU had been used to. It emphasized the US's national interests and imposed tariffs on European goods. The TTIP free trade agreement, which had been jointly planned for many years, disappeared long ago from the media and public debate. And the US's expectation that its European allies will invest more in their own defense is creating new security policy challenges. In contrast to the EU's relations with the US, those with Canada remain stable. That can be seen, for example, in the Comprehensive Economic and Trade Agreement (CETA) that was signed at the EU-Canada Summit on October 30, 2016. Yet it is still true that, by working together, America and Europe could achieve much more and could promote their shared values and interests. For that to happen, Europe must continue to develop and must learn to stand more on its own feet and take responsibility.

The EU and Its Neighbors: A Ring of Fire and Conflicts

2016

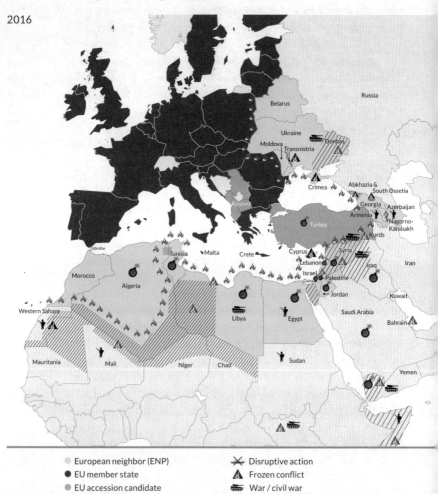

● European neighbor (ENP)	✕ Disruptive action
● EU member state	⚠ Frozen conflict
● EU accession candidate	🛡 War / civil war

Source: Bertelsmann Stiftung 2016 and 2021

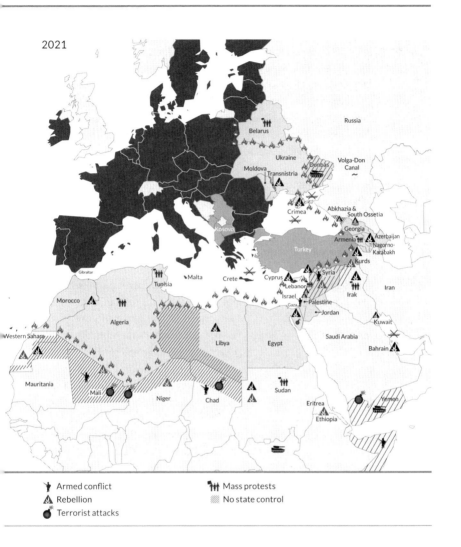

2021

Russia
Belarus
Ukraine
Moldova
Transnistria
Donbas
Volga-Don Canal
Crimea
Abkhazia & South Ossetia
Kosovo
Georgia
Armenia
Azerbaijan
Turkey
Nagorno-Karabakh
Kurds
Gibraltar
Tunisia
Malta
Crete
Cyprus
Syria
Iran
Lebanon
Irak
Morocco
Israel
Palestine
Gaza
Jordan
Algeria
Kuwait
Western Sahara
Libya
Egypt
Saudi Arabia
Bahrain
Mauritania
Mali
Niger
Chad
Sudan
Yemen
Eritrea
Ethiopia

Armed conflict
Mass protests
Rebellion
No state control
Terrorist attacks

Relations between Russia and the EU have been strongly affected in recent years by the annexation of Crimea and the resulting conflict in eastern Ukraine. Opinion among member states on the Nord Stream 2 pipeline is divided, showing the political limits of the EU's own role. Moreover, Russia's involvement in the civil wars in Syria and Libya has complicated political relations. Although Russia and the EU have close economic ties – Russia's economic performance is highly dependent on oil and gas prices – the EU, together with other Western states, has regularly extended the sanctions imposed on Russia since 2014. High inflation, falling oil prices and massive capital flight are further burdens on the Russian economy. Although tensions are increasing between Russia and the EU, it is imperative that the two partners do not turn away from each other. Preventing this might be difficult, time-consuming and strenuous, but it is worth the effort.

After all, it is pointless to isolate and exclude neighboring countries – and Russia remains an important neighbor for Europe. Dialogue on Russia's internal situation will therefore continue to be an important issue. Without Russia and its influence, it will be much more difficult to achieve constructive goals and overcome challenges. Lest we forget, we are talking about a member of the UN Security Council with veto power. Europe's role will thus depend on political realpolitik, but also on how it deals with key global players.

The People's Republic of China has long been one of the European Union's most important trading partners. The EU imports more goods from China than it does from the US, although it exports less to the People's Republic than it imports in return. This has led to a trade deficit with China, even if the EU has a surplus when it comes to services. The EU's trade with China is also likely to develop far more dynamically in the next 10 years (growing 80 percent) than with the US (30 percent). Europe and China therefore face more shared challenges than they are willing to admit. Historically, China and the EU experienced a similar rise – for which the EU required almost 70 years while China needed less than 40. The dynamism and expansion of world trade can be seen here as reinforcing factors. In the meantime, close partnerships have developed in the areas of climate protection, trade, investment and education. However, foreign policy relations between the EU and the People's Republic have been very ambivalent over the years.

On the one hand, there have been efforts on both sides to expand economic relations. The linking of a "European silk road" with China's existing Belt and Road Initiative would be beneficial not only for the EU and China, but also for the regions in between. On the other hand, various topics have presented themselves, especially recently, that require discussion. China's neighbors, for example, are concerned about its hegemonic power, fearing a military build-up and regional conflicts. The focus has repeatedly been on the situation in the South China Sea, where maritime boundaries remain in dispute. There are also numerous questions for which the EU has tried to find answers in the past, and continues to do so today: How should Chinese companies be approached given concerns about "infrastructure security"? How should the EU react to the suppression of the democracy movement in Hong Kong or to accusations that China is discriminating against and persecuting Uighurs? What can be done to protect European firms from cyberattacks and patent infringement? Can the EU maintain a neutral position in the trade war between China and the US and resist being instrumentalized?

Thus, the European Union faces the major challenge of finding an appropriate position vis-à-vis the People's Republic. It will be necessary to ensure a balance is struck between maintaining relations, both political and economic, and asserting European values. In particular, the Chinese government's response to the Covid-19 pandemic, which originated in China, is bound to have long-lasting consequences for bilateral relations.

Europe and the Trilogue Salzburg

The role of Europe was and is the recurring focus of the Trilogue Salzburg. The international exchange of ideas that takes place at the gathering has made it possible to examine European challenges from different perspectives using a multilateral lens. The Trilogue's strength is building bridges, even across different viewpoints. That has always meant bringing people together across countries, continents, languages and backgrounds, and using conversations and discussions to identify approaches that can unite us regardless of borders. The key has been considering different perspectives from the political, business and cultural spheres in order to examine Europe's far-reaching, multifaceted role.

Early on it became clear that Europe and the European Union are at a crossroads and that we urgently need to ask ourselves which European future we envision. At one of the first Trilogues, for example, our deliberations focused on Europe's global responsibility. This quintessential issue is timelier than ever: There is too little political unity, emotional appeal or military might behind the European idea for Europe to play a real role or assume responsibility geopolitically. Moreover, Europe is not curious enough about the changes taking place in the world and indulges in eurocentrism instead. Back then, the current president of the German Bundestag, Wolfgang Schäuble, pointed out that Europe can only tackle these challenges within a close transatlantic partnership. It is not a matter of a specifically European message, he said, but a message from the entire Western world, which now faces global challenges. The Spanish composer and conductor Cristóbal Halffter felt Europe's main task was to contribute its values and cultural achievements to the dialogue of civilizations. This is particularly true in terms of the civilizations that did not experience the Enlightenment, he said, and it is where Europe must advocate for a humanistic world view, gender equality, separation of church and state, and human rights.

The extent to which Asia's rise would serve as a stabilizing factor for the global economy while also confronting the global community with major political challenges was already an issue in 2006 when the Trilogue examined "Asia's New Powers – Repercussions for Europe." The participants agreed that shaping effective responses to the attendant challenges meant engaging more deeply with Asia not only on an economic front, but also in terms of politics, culture and religion. Former European Commissioner for Competition Peter Sutherland noted that integration is part of the answer and not part of the problem, saying, "If we impair or stop the process, Europe will be incapable of shaping globalization and will suffer long-term repercussions as a result." Back then as well, Victor Chu, chairman of First Eastern Investment Group, emphasized Europe's groundbreaking role and the European idea's exemplary nature for regional integration efforts, including for Asia.

The substantive focus, which draws decision makers from around the world to Salzburg, shows the importance of the yearly exchange on issues impacting the globe's future. Speaking at the Trilogue many years ago, Martin Lees, former secretary general of the Club of Rome, pointed out that we cannot view problems in isolation, but must be aware of how much all problems and tasks are interconnected, even if many in the European Union were closing their eyes to various crises.

That is why, since 2013, Trilogue participants have summarized the results of their discussions as the "Salzburg Recommendations," which are made available to the European Commission, the Council of the European Union and the EU member states. With that, the Trilogue Salzburg provides an ongoing platform for discussions of Europe's role. The thoughts expressed in Salzburg thus make it possible to reflect on a "New Europe" – i.e. on a shared, new narrative.

For example, the 15th Trilogue Salzburg was dedicated to the topic "Neighbourhood Policy and Regional Integration," inspired by the common European Neighbourhood Policy (ENP) first developed by the EU in 2004. Back then, changing political and economic realities and increasing instability and armed conflicts were the reasons, as they still are today, for reassessing relations with neighbors. Countries and regions located directly across the border play a special role, since resolving conflicts there is usually more pressing and must include various interest groups. In light of that, economic stimulation and cooperation with certain regions can only succeed in an environment offering long-term stability.

The 2016 Trilogue Salzburg showed that the ENP urgently needed realigning. The reason was the series of trouble spots stretching from North Africa to Ukraine, encircling the European community and forming a "ring of fire." Yet dealing with neighbors is not always easy. After all, unlike trading partners, neighbors cannot be chosen. During the event, participants evaluated the historical and current relationships of the three global players – the US, China and the EU – with their neighbors. Recommendations were then formulated showing how it would be possible to reestablish a "ring of friends," as existed at the beginning of the 21st century:

- The European Union and China have numerous, highly diverse neighboring states which cannot be dealt with using a one-size-fits-all approach, as with the ENP. The regional context must continue to be taken into account, so that individual interests and needs can continue to be met.
- Depending on the state of bilateral relations, developments often occur that bring neighborhood policy into sharper focus. Issues must be prioritized in a coordinated manner if the relevant programs and policies are to be beneficial for both sides.
- The instruments that exist for implementing neighborhood policy, such as bilateral trade agreements and security measures, remain important, but must be improved and supplemented by new instruments, such as educational partnerships or cultural exchange programs, as a way of promoting mutual understanding.
- Certain developments, such as the Arab Spring, the influx of refugees and migrants, Brexit, and the terrorist attacks in Europe's major cities, have often come as a surprise in the past and have had a large impact on Europe's role in the world. Developments in neighboring countries must therefore be examined in greater detail so that fundamental changes can be recognized early on.

Five years after these recommendations were made, the EU still faces numerous expectations about what its role should be from allies, trading partners and others around the world with whom it has cooperative relationships. Old challenges persist, such as Brexit, the fight against climate change, the conflicts in eastern Ukraine, Syria's civil war and China's maneuvers in the South China Sea. New challenges include internal disputes over rule of law in European countries, such as Poland and Hungary, and, since 2019, the Covid-19 pandemic. Which developments will occur in light of the new presidential administration in the US and the slightly improved refugee situation is as yet an open question. Against this background, it can be assumed that the aforementioned recommendations are still valid and will remain so going forward.

Ultimately, Europe must learn to live with crises and, despite all adversities, maintain a dialogue – in some cases with individuals and organizations with whom dialogue hardly seems imaginable.

Only through a common stance, common interests and mutual trust will Europe be able to respond effectively to these challenges and thus create a New Europe. The Trilogue Salzburg was, is and will be an event that focuses on Europe. And by developing recommendations for overcoming global challenges, it can help shape this vision of a New Europe.

ÖSTERREICH — ein paar Anregunge

100

bei Stau-
Flugauto, 2032
von DigiTechUni Linz
entwickelt...

EU-

Aussengrenz-
schutz

EWR
Mittelmeer

2010

getrennte Fahrbahnen
LKW's & PKW's

Finanz-
Transaktions-
steuer

NEURO

getrennte Trinkwasser-
und Brauchwasser-
Leitungen

2030

EU-Peace
Corps

Banken-
Union

EU-Verteidigg.
gemeinsam

gemein
Luftrau
schutz
Mitteleuro

4% F&E

STADTSCHLÜSSEL
der ersten Neugründung
der ersten hundert Jahren
seit Tullnerfeld
in Tullnerfeld
(für den Namen d. Neustadt
(auf Internet-Abstimmung)
2035

Wiener
Philharmoniker
+ Regierung gründen
Musikschulen in
Krisengebieten...
(und jeder Ve
kann läuft ei

spielt alle
Studin: Digital,
Erneuerb.Energie,
öffts.Nahversorg,
Architektur,

FESTSPIELE

202 Salzburg wird
zum Davos der
KULTUR

122 Jah

Thoughts on Europe's Role in the World

Ursula Plassnik
Austrian Diplomat and Politician

Where do you see Europe in coming years in terms of the balance of power with the US, China and Russia?

> *The European Union offers more than 450 million people a shared space for democracy, rule of law and respect for diversity. The EU is the world's largest contributor of development aid. It is increasingly becoming a global standard-setter when it comes to human rights, fair competition, data protection, product safety and environmental standards. Where other powers focus on military security, Europe relies on the power of its unique combination of freedom, security and solidarity. That is what makes Europe so attractive for people from all around the world. Europe is redefining the concept of power.*

What has to happen for Europe to (again) become a global player?

> *The EU must work on its strategic autonomy. And promote a modern concept of sovereignty, one that is democratic, cooperative, liberal – more 21st century than the classic model from the 19th century. There's also room for improvement in the EU's political marketing. As a famous American journalist noted, Europe is the world's worst-marketed political miracle.*

What is Europe's shared story today?

As a continent that was torn apart for centuries by war and violence, Europe today is a pioneer in the area of peaceful cooperation and competition. Brexit and the Covid-19 pandemic have shown the distress resulting from "non-Europe." Despite all our cherished differences, we Europeans have achieved a remarkable degree of shared identity.

20 years of the Trilogue Salzburg: What was your "Trilogue moment"?

The story of the Trilogue began back in the 1990s, in the pre-Bertelsmann Stiftung era. In keeping with family tradition, Wolfgang Schüssel, then Austria's foreign minister and vice-chancellor, always spent part of the summer in the Salzkammergut region. As a musician, he was passionately interested in the performing arts and was therefore a frequent visitor to the Salzburg Festival. As his chief of staff, I was tasked with establishing a new platform where leading figures from politics, business and the arts would come together to exchange views on current topics. German philosopher Peter Sloterdijk was one of the first participants, as was the mayor of Venice, Massimo Caccari, and the singers Thomas Hampson, Helen Donath, Michael Schade and Waltraud Mayer. "Busting silos," the Trilogue's basic principle, is timelier and more pressing than ever!

Europe's Economy as the Focus of Discussion

Europe can be more than a little proud of its economic record. The postwar boom brought an unusual level of growth to the continent's western regions, along with substantial increases in income accompanied by advances in technology and development. At least until the oil shock, economic developments only seemed to move in one direction thanks to Europe's integration into free trade flows, as well as greater European cooperation, boosts in productivity and modernized manufacturing processes. Moreover, the Council for Mutual Economic Assistance (COMECON), which was founded in response to the Marshall Plan, was meant to ensure planned growth, promote industrial development and increase production in Eastern Europe, in addition to furthering socialistic economic integration. The resulting division of the continent and the competition between both systems left their mark on entire generations and culminated in the thesis advanced by Francis Fukuyama, which held that, following the collapse of the Eastern bloc, the principles of liberalism in the form of democracy and a market economy would prevail everywhere and forevermore.

Indisputably, this era bestowed on Europe a previously unknown level of prosperity. Yet the diminishing increases in production, the market saturation and the social and environmental impacts of the ever-greater push for growth also showed that economic activity has its limits. Failures such as the financial and economic crisis, the banking crisis, market bubbles, competition for resources, and the ecological consequences of short-term thinking have made it clear to everyone how easily the global economy can slip out of balance.

These events demonstrate the need to have an appropriate framework for economic activity in place and to ensure that Europe is home to a sustainable economic order. Yet they also show the deficits in current modes of thinking, to the extent that inequality is increasing on a national and international level, and the question must be posed of whether humanity's consumption of natural resources is too great for the planet to sustain.

The "European Dream"

Short-term thinking and an insufficient sense of responsibility have not only resulted in problems, but also in the loss of what binds society together: trust and values! Many people are increasingly seeing that material well-being and growth are not everything and that the market cannot fix it all by itself. People expect the state and the government to intervene. But under what conditions should such an intervention take place? Is the European economy sustainable if it no longer generates economic growth? Do we need successful markets before we start thinking about creating an ethically acceptable market economy?

It is not only about growth, jobs and technological progress, but about carefully weighing the consequences of Europe's actions. Sufficient growth, however, will be the key to many things – including innovation, research, education and infrastructure. It is also a question of how Europe wants to do business in the future. Like the American Dream, don't we also need a slogan that brings Europeans together? What might a "European Dream" look like that is worth living and working for?

It must certainly be based on the unexceptional term "growth." Since more goods are produced and more services used, growth is often automatically equated with more prosperity. The next conclusion is often: More prosperity equals more quality of life. Or in other words: Growth is the key to satisfaction and happiness. People want progress – and they want to do their bit to achieve it. Yes, they want growth – but not at any price! We see the boom in the emerging economies, but we also see the social inequality. The world is undergoing radical change. How can we successfully manage that change?

Social Justice (2019) and GDP per Capita (2018)

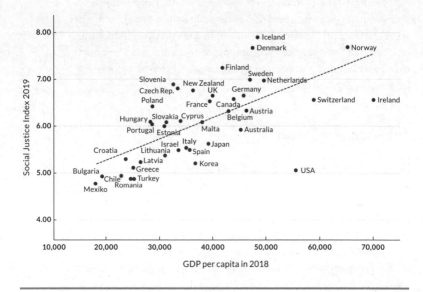

Source: Bertelsmann Stiftung (2019). *Social Justice in the EU and OECD. Index Report 2019.* Gütersloh. p. 11.

The pillars of the European economy

Growth has not always emerged from the European continent alone, and it has not always given rise to social participation. Many politicians and business leaders have acted and continue to act only in their own interests or those of their nation. It is apparent that our consumption of resources takes place at the detriment of others. At least since the beginning of the colonial era, it has been clear that Europe's strengths can be traced back to the resources it has acquired (and appropriated) from other countries. In striving for growth, we are increasingly living at the expense of coming generations, something that applies to the world's richer nations in particular. The consequences – high government debt, climate change and unemployment, along with social inequality – are the greatest threats to peace in the world.

People must be prepared not only for individual reforms, but for real change – in societal as well as environmental terms. These two points will be crucial for determining how we do business. At the same time, we cannot forget that even today our economy is based primarily on past growth, massive human capital, and the preservation and creation of new knowledge. Living in the age of globalization is apparently much more difficult than we thought. Perhaps we underestimated it.

Today's megatrends continue to influence how robust these pillars will be in the future. For example, global trade has become an integral part of the economy, and rising exports are altering the current-account balances of many trading partners. Linked production sites are determining the length of trading routes and of supply and value chains. Global financial markets are accelerating global trade and facilitating numerous direct investments. Many companies have become global players that can manufacture and sell their products all around the globe.

Yet the unequal distribution of global resources is also impacting the lives of many people. Greater inequality and repression are jeopardizing democracy and market economies worldwide. The current Bertelsmann Transformation Index (BTI) shows that more and more democracies are experiencing a decline in rule of law and political freedom. The causes are clientelism, nepotism and the concentration of power, as well as policy actors' inability to solve problems and achieve compromise. For example, poverty and inequality are widespread in 76 out of 137 countries, including 46 of 50 African states. A key question seems to be: How can we create the right framework for the entrepreneurship and creative freedoms that counteract a weakening of democracy? That will determine whether we can compete globally in the long term.

Overview of the Transformation Processes in 137 Developing
and Transition Countries

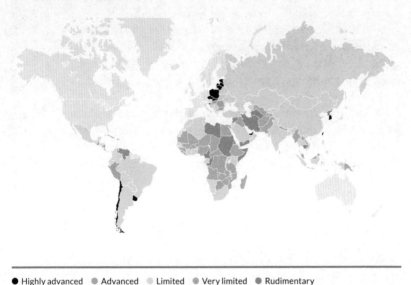

● Highly advanced   ● Advanced   ● Limited   ● Very limited   ● Rudimentary

Source: Bertelsmann Stiftung (2020). *Transformation Index – BTI 2020*. Gütersloh. pp. 22–23.

Cohesion in the face of shared challenges

The pandemic is showing how crisis-prone such a networked global economy is. We are experiencing first-hand the dangers stemming from a global virus and its impact on politics, business and society. The measures adopted to curb transmission have interrupted supply changes, businesses have had to close temporarily and, because of lockdowns, people have had to remain mostly at home. Economic performance has slumped worldwide and Europe has entered a recession that is deeper than the one that followed the 2008 economic and financial crisis.

At the same time, we are witnessing global cooperation among researchers as we combat the virus. These are times that will go down in history. Yet how that history will be written is up to us. We can decide today how we want to shape tomorrow. It is time to develop responses that can build a sustainable market economy – an economic order that will turn not only Europe, but the whole world into a place where coming generations will also have a seat at the table. Numerous challenges will have to be overcome, however, as we work towards that goal. We now have the possibility of deploying new ideas and innovations to model options for society's future – across national borders and cultures. Shouldn't we also view the crisis as an opportunity to strike out in a new direction?

We are at a turning point – due to globalization, but also due to digitalization. Their ramifications for the economy and society have never been more pronounced and are changing all our lives. The pace at which technology is developing is now faster than the speed at which governments, regulators and businesses can adjust to the new realities. Not too long ago, young founders arrived from Silicon Valley to preach the virtues of technological progress; today, they face critical questions. The optimism of the early years has dissipated and, in some cases, has even turned into the opposite – thanks to fake news, cyberattacks and the general feeling of technological overload.

Yet isn't feeling overwhelmed by and distrustful of technological progress the sign of a larger problem? Isn't it more disturbing that there are hardly any large European companies driving digitalization in the various European countries? Consider, for example, the renowned European firms, such as Nokia, Motorola and Nixdorf, that didn't succeed in undergoing the necessary transformation. How is the European economy responding to digitalization and how is it shaping it? American and Asian companies still seem to be the ones accomplishing that task. When an enterprise adept at digitalization miraculously appears in Europe, it is quickly acquired by a foreign investor. The international competition that European companies could engage in ends before it has even begun.

Critical voices are already claiming that the European business community has failed when it comes to digitalization and is no longer competitive. But it's not enough to constantly complain about what Europe has failed to do. Europe must play to its strengths; after all, the competition is not standing idly by – not in the US, China or Russia, and not the predominant tech giants. A single market must also be created in the area of digitalization, and a sensible balance must be found between innovation, on the one hand, and data and privacy protection, on the other. Thus, in

Digitalization in EU countries according to the 2020 DESI Index

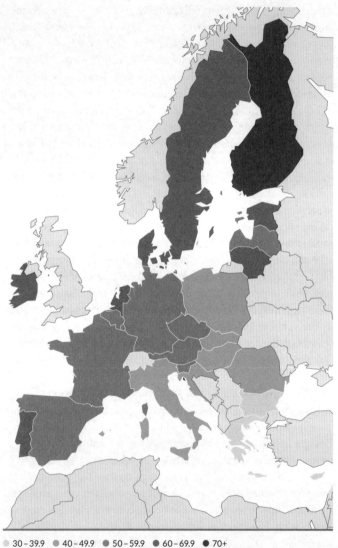

● 30–39.9 ● 40–49.9 ● 50–59.9 ● 60–69.9 ● 70+

Sum of the results for the dimensions "Connectivity," "Human Capital," "Internet Usage," "Integration of Digital Technology" and "Digital Public Services"; max. score: 100 points

Source: European Commission (2020). Digital Economy and Society Index (DESI) 2020. https://digital-strategy.ec.europa.eu/en/policies/desi; authors' calculations.

terms of its digital future, Europe has to take existing norms and values into account, without missing out on important opportunities to develop or being left behind in the competition with other global regions.

The source of this problem can be seen when companies are first launched. Even small start-ups face completely different conditions in European countries than in the US, Israel or China. A key factor here is the funding available to such young, high-risk enterprises. There seems to be much room for expansion in Europe's venture capital and private equity sectors, a situation that especially benefits risk-friendly global players. In its project "Repair and Prepare: Strengthening Europe," the Bertelsmann Stiftung has ascertained that traditional goals such as size and growth are almost out of reach for European start-ups. It would therefore make sense to pool innovative resources in order to jointly overcome societal challenges. Creativity, passion and drive, and not least courage – those are qualities that illustrious managers have often exhibited when creating successful enterprises. Aren't they also the qualities that society urgently needs in view of the many global challenges it faces?

Another driver of future challenges is demographic change. This means Europe will be home to fewer and fewer young, qualified workers in coming years. As a result, it will have to compete for them on the international job market. When choosing a job, young people today increasingly look at what a potential employer can offer in terms of environmental protection and sustainability. Carsharing, train passes and financial assistance for purchasing an e-bike have long ceased to be unusual as perks. Thus, the pressure that European companies face to do more for the environment no longer comes only externally from policy makers and NGOs, but also internally from employees.

Greater requirements to protect the climate and the efforts needed to comply with them are, however, not possible without increased spending on climate-friendly alternatives. That means, in the short term, European companies could find themselves at a disadvantage relative to competitors who can produce more cheaply in regions without such requirements. Yet is this a reason to continue on as before? Is a business's sole purpose to maximize profits for

OECD States and 20 Countries with the Lowest Median Age

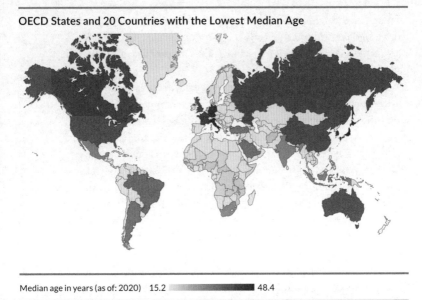

Median age in years (as of: 2020)   15.2 ▮▮▮▮▮▮▮▮▮ 48.4

Source: Deutsche Stiftung Weltbevölkerung (2020). *DSW-Datenreport 2020*. Hannover. pp. 8–17.

its shareholders? Shouldn't companies contribute to society as well? It's possible that the effort to realize new, climate-friendly alternatives could strengthen Europe's innovative power and thus its economy in the long run.

Policy makers' responsibility

Europe's economy and growth lie not only in the hands of companies and the business community – it is urgent that policy makers also discuss the issue. The latter are now called upon to do what is right in a changing world. Ultimately, policy measures will play a decisive role in how the European economy develops in the future. After all, when the economy is functioning as it should, democracy has an easier time of it and people need not go hungry. Yet when political systems fail – due to corruption, for example – the economy cannot function. And where there are no laws at all, people starve and life is violent – and there can be no growth.

One of the originators of the European idea, Robert Schuman, said that there are always two main forces in politics: the power of fear and the power of hope. We must overcome the "yes, but" and the many small objections that prevail in politics – otherwise the framework conditions will be set by others. To that end, we need good policies and good explanations – among other reasons, to take the wind out of the sails of populists.

The goal of political activity is usually economic growth. This applies to individual European countries and – often – to the European Union. A crucial factor here is the rise or fall in the gross domestic product (GDP) of the countries (or groups thereof) in question. The assumption is that when a country experiences strong economic growth, there will also be social justice and prosperity for its citizens. A suitable economic policy therefore uses incentives (subsidies) or prohibitions (laws) to set framework conditions that ultimately affect the entire European economy. International free trade agreements like CETA, the failed TTIP agreement and efforts to create a new Silk Road are also economic policy undertakings that can have far-reaching consequences.

In a globally interconnected world, these and other problems cannot be solved by individual countries, but only through global cooperation. Around the world, political, business and civil society actors are confronted with complex challenges. That means responsibility must be assumed – through leadership. Yet as the world around us changes, how leadership is defined is also changing. Which means the standards leaders must meet are changing as well – whether those leaders are active in the political, economic or cultural spheres. The demands made of people and, with that, the burdens they bear are becoming more complex.

One Belt, One Road Region

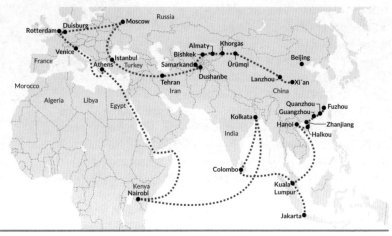

■■■ New Silk Road　　■■■ Maritime Silk Road

Source: Sander Denecker (2015). "China's 'One Belt One Road' Strategy." https://www.amcham-shanghai.org/en/article/chinas-one-belt-one-road-strategy

The increase in international agreements and treaties is giving rise to a more open market economy with almost innumerable actors. Myriad government and nongovernmental organizations are active on the international level, thereby influencing the economy. Political reporting in particular often focuses on the short term and individual events. We see paradigm-shifting improvements, but also devastating natural catastrophes, atrocities in Syria, problems in Ukraine, political and social tensions in the US, which attract the attention of people around the globe for a short while.

The importance of intercultural exchange and education

Many challenges must be addressed through a dialogue among political, economic and cultural actors. This includes relearning how to share. As we all know from personal experience, few things are as motivating as the feeling of having reached a major goal on one's own. Equally important, however, are role models and pioneers who point the way. Mutual trust and respect for people and cultures are also crucial. Anyone can become a role model for others through his or her attitudes and the beliefs he or she lives. Every dialogue is a bridge across societal gridlock. Moreover, people must be allowed to make mistakes – otherwise they can never learn how to be enterprising and take responsibility.

In terms of educational policy, schools and training centers must continue to be optimized in order to avert the impending shortage of skilled workers. New technologies are creating many new possibilities – and gradually bringing the world closer together. Education must become more digital. It can network knowledge to the greatest extent possible – for our globalized future. Thanks to the Internet, we can now bring education to the most remote villages at very little cost. We cannot allow today's students to be prepared for tomorrow's problems in yesterday's schools by teachers from the day before yesterday using methods from past centuries. Some European countries have become pioneers here; the Covid-19 pandemic has also helped digitalize education. Yet there is still plenty of room for improvement.

Above all, Europe's diverse university landscape can serve as a driving force for the economy. For example, in Europe more women than men complete a tertiary degree. That's good news, even if the figures vary considerably from country to country. Many women and men are still fighting for recognition, as well as better working conditions and possibilities for achieving work-life balance. Here, too, policy makers are called upon to turn Europe into a forward-looking place where competition among researchers generates additional innovations and, at the same time, resources are pooled so people can work together on solutions.

Something that cannot be neglected are the cultural influences that have had an ever greater impact on the European economy in recent decades. They allow us to learn with and from each other – so we can set the course for a future worth living. Promoting education and knowledge across borders is and will remain our only possibility to make the world more social, just and peaceful.

International tourism has grown continuously over the past decades, and Europe has proven to be the most popular destination. In 2018, half of the foreign tourists visiting the EU travelled to Spain

(23%), Italy (16%) or France (11%), making the economy and the people there very dependent on tourism. In a globally networked world, foreign languages are also becoming more important. Yet the influence of individual countries has also become apparent here: English is now an integral part of the business world and can be considered the Internet's "native language."

Rethinking business in Salzburg

Given all these challenges, the Trilogue's discussions have repeatedly focused on the topic of "business in Europe." On the one hand, the growing scarcity of resources, the threats to the environment, and hunger, poverty and war all reveal the limits Europe's economic actors face. On the other hand, without a market economy, innovation and entrepreneurship, growth and thus progress on the continent would, presumably, quickly reach their own limits. To what extent will the global and European economic systems thus remain viable over time? And is a radically new approach needed so people do not continue to do business at the expense of coming generations? For three consecutive years we looked exclusively and intensively at these questions. First, there was the 2010 Trilogue on "Perspectives on Qualitative Growth from Europe, the Black Sea Region and Beyond." What seemed promising at the time was the creation of a future-ready social market economy designed to influence people's behavior in a positive way. The core objective formulated back then is timelier than ever: In the future, economic growth must be more socially and ecologically acceptable and must reflect both people's needs and the fact that resources are limited.

No one wants to prevent emerging economies from reaching the standards and quality of life found in Western societies. Yet it is in everybody's interest that others do not repeat the mistakes made by the first societies to industrialize in terms of their use of resources and promotion of inequality. As investor Victor Chu from Hong Kong warned back then: "Humanity has shown again and again that it can respond constructively to the challenges of its time. Whenever limits were reached, people found solutions. But the situation in our globalized world, which is expected to have nine billion inhabitants by the year 2050, has become so complex, that I seriously wonder if humanity is creative enough to meet all of these needs. What happens if our creativity is not sufficient to come up with the necessary solutions?"

Against the background of the financial crisis, there was widespread agreement in 2010 that precisely the world economy's most globalized industry, the financial sector, was still a black hole, albeit one that should not be over-regulated. What was crucial, participants at the event agreed, was that even though we had learned from earlier upheavals, we had yet to draw any lessons from the current one. At the same time, it was clear that the world needed to be prepared for the next crisis. For the then director-general of the World Trade Organization, Pascal Lamy, that meant "globally, we don't need more power for governments, but more and clear rules." Regulation that is tied to national interests is incapable of creating a global commonweal, he said, and the future of the market economy depends on maintaining boundaries, promoting participation and securing quality of life for everyone. That is what would show, Lamy explained, if the right lessons had been learned from the recent crisis.

Such an "ethical market economy" is predicated on an image of humanity which is no longer striving for material benefits, but increasingly for the nonmaterial values of well-being, such as health, social relationships and recognition. This requires a multidimensional definition of social progress and prosperity. The long-outmoded indicator of GDP needs to be supplemented by welfare indicators, thus making it easier to measure whether social and environmental goals have been achieved. Austria's then Foreign Minister Michael Spindelegger called for the development of "broader measures of welfare" at the European level that target social and ecological goals in addition to economic output. They are an important tool, he said, to align economic growth with people's true needs and to demonstrate successes in decoupling from energy and resource consumption. The political and economic spheres must therefore reestablish a dialogue with the public as a way of regaining the trust that has been lost through the years.

Building on this, the challenges of global governance were discussed one year later at the 10th Trilogue Salzburg. Long before

French Foreign Minister Jean-Yves Le Drian and his German counterpart Heiko Maas launched the Alliance for Multilateralism in 2019, the problem of supranational policy had already been on the agenda in the city of Mozart's birth. Multilateralism in its existing form no longer works and what would be helpful is not more consensus, but more convergence, said Dino Djalal, founder of the Foreign Policy Community of Indonesia. Based on the principle of consensus, global politics is incapable of managing complex global problems and systemic risks, he explained, nor can it prevent overuse of the global commons or internalize the serious external costs of increasing consumption by the world's constantly growing population.

New approaches are urgently needed to manage the world economy with its conflicting interests, systemic risks and social and environmental costs, Djalal explained. The structural reforms usually discussed in the relevant institutions are no longer sufficient, he said. More important is a new "software" capable of making the priorities visible that the global economy should meet, as well as the rules that could be used to resolve conflicts between actors and interests on the global level. He noted that an important step towards a less crisis-prone world economy would be a charter of sustainable economic activity jointly developed by Western and non-Western actors, one that describes in comprehensible language which economic, ecological and social goals are to be pursued globally using which policy measures.

As the French anthropologist Marc Abélès pointed out, these goals cannot be imposed top-down, but must be derived from the world views of people all around the globe and from their expectations for the future. "That is the reason why, as a solution for regulatory problems, a kind of charter must be created, a description in simple, politically understandable terms of how we want to deal with globalization and its challenges. Let's approach the problem in this way, knowing that such a process will call into question some of current system's Western ideological foundations," said WTO President Lamy. "As long as we do not have such a normative framework showing what we want to achieve together – and possibly differently than before – we will have to continue to make due with a very low level of political will. We will continue to hear a lot of talk about the failures of policy leadership. That's okay, but calling for leadership in a vacuum doesn't work. It's meaningless. There is no failure to lead when people do not hold their leaders accountable for reaching goals. We must finally move forward."

From there it was only a short step to the 2012 Trilogue, which was dedicated to the topic "Tackling the Global Gordian Knot: Can Economic Growth Be Socially Inclusive and Environmentally Sustainable?" During the gathering, participants discussed the challenges and strategies related to global economic growth. They called for switching from a growth-based to a development-based approach that gives top priority to combatting poverty and promoting education while guaranteeing access to clean energy. According to many of those present, multilateral organizations have shown themselves to be unsuitable platforms for reaching an international consensus. What is needed, they said, is a "coalition of the willing" consisting of governments, businesses and civil society actors who would contribute their – potentially groundbreaking – experiences and visions on the policy level.

Participants also expressed clear criticism of exaggerated expectations of growth. As then Slovakian Prime Minister Iveta Radicova put it, "We have to tell the truth. Forget growth. We are all in debt, and in the middle of a recession. The current growth model can't be maintained in its current form." The participants in Salzburg cautioned that the debt problem should be monitored instead, otherwise, among other crises, hyperinflation and stagflation could ensue, as in South America.

In many countries economic growth is still seen as a necessary condition for political and social stability – hence the importance of developing sustainable growth drivers. Moreover, social inequality and the ongoing depletion of natural resources are challenges that multilateral organizations repeatedly fail to address due to a lack of consensus. The recommendations developed as a result of the above include:

- Define benchmarks and goals, including specific timeframes and standards, that serve as incentives for sustainable behavioral change
- Measure the externalities of economic growth

- Promote close cooperation between the public sector, the business community and civil society
- View regional organizations (e.g. the BRICS countries) as pioneers in the area of multilateral initiatives
- Develop a charter of "global rights" and "sustainable development goals" comparable to the Millennium Development Goals that include the right to education, access to clean energy and water, and the prospect of employment
- Design new indicators that do not measure prosperity based only on GDP, but also on consumption, income and quality of life
- Assemble "coalitions of the willing / of progressive minorities" consisting of governments, businesses and civil society institutions that can lead the way by contributing their visions and experiences in the policy sphere

Thoughts on Europe's Economy – Competitiveness, Sustainability and Globalization

Pascal Lamy
Former European Commissioner for Trade and
Director-General of the World Trade Organization

How competitive is the European economy? What opportunities are there, and what risks?

> *If you look at the trade surplus, the EU can be considered quite competitive. However, our comparative advantage is higher in the old economy than in the new one. That's a serious risk for the future which we must address.*

What kind of growth should Europe strive for?

> *Challenge No. 1 for the EU's economy is decarbonization. Reaching the agreed goals (net zero emissions by 2050 and, as an interim target, a 55% reduction by 2030) will require massive effort and changes to our systems of production and consumption. And that will entail new challenges in the area of innovation as well as new societal risks.*

Is Europe's prosperity at risk? If so, what must we do to prevent an economic decline?

> *Prosperity in the EU is not having an easy go of it considering the demographic figures, e.g. the shrinking and aging population. And the EU's ability to maintain its relatively generous social welfare systems – which must remain a hallmark of European civilization*

in the world – is getting shaky. The only thing that can compensate for this handicap is higher productivity, most of which will have to come from innovation. That's why our top priority should be reclaiming the ground we've lost on a number of technological fronts.

20 years of the Trilogue Salzburg: What was your "Trilogue moment"?

My best Trilogue moments in Salzburg were the ones in which artists were part of the discussions, since they brought openness, ideas, dreams and observations to the debates. They thereby moved the usual friendly suspects beyond their comfort zone in an interesting and effective way, as the latter attempted to reshape Europe and the world.

Photo Gallery: 20 Years
of the Trilogue Salzburg

from left: Aleksander Kwaśniewski (President of the Republic of Poland), Liz Mohn, Wolfgang Schüssel

Participants in the first Trilogue Salzburg in 2004, from left:
Helga Rabl-Stadler (President of the Salzburg Festival),
Prince El Hassan bin Talal (President of the Club of Rome),
Wolfgang Schüssel, Pascal Lamy (European Commissioner for Trade)

Wolfgang Schüssel playing on Mozart's
original instrument

from left: Lorenz Tomerius (Berlin-based culture journalist), Liz Mohn,
Wolfgang Schüssel

Liz Mohn and Wolfgang Schüssel

Wolfgang Schäuble (Deputy Chairman of the CDU/CSU Group
in the German Bundestag for Foreign, Security and European Policy),
Ursula Plassnik (Foreign Minister of the Republic of Austria)

Participants in the 2005 Trilogue Salzburg

Dieter H. Vogel (Chairman of the Bertelsmann Stiftung Board of Trustees) and Jürgen Strube (Chairman of the BASF AG Supervisory Board)

Wolfgang Schüssel and Liz Mohn

Yue Sai Kan (Chinese television host and producer) and Liz Mohn

Discussion at the 2006 Trilogue Salzburg

Liz Mohn, Bianca Jagger (Nicaraguan-British human rights activist)

Liz Mohn, Jürgen Flimm (German stage director, actor, theater manager and university instructor)

from left: Victor L. L. Chu (Chairman and CEO of First Eastern Investment Group), Liz Mohn and Wolfgang Schüssel

Wolfgang Schüssel speaking with school students

Daniel Barenboim (Argentinian-Israeli pianist and conductor),
Michael Spindelegger (Foreign Minister of the Republic of Austria)

from left: Wolfgang Schüssel, Margit and Michael Spindelegger
(Foreign Minister of the Republic of Austria), Liz Mohn,
Gunter Thielen (Chairman of the Bertelsmann AG Supervisory Board)

from left: Nicolas Berggruen (German-American investor),
Michael Spindelegger (Foreign Minister of the Republic of Austria),
Liz Mohn, Wolfgang Schüssel

Dennis Snower (President of the Institute for the World Economy)

from left: Jörg Dräger (Member of the Bertelsmann Stiftung Executive Board), Wolfgang Aulitzky (President of the American Austrian Foundation), Liz Mohn, Helga Rabl-Stadler (President of the Salzburg Festival), Wolfgang Schüssel

from left: Wolfgang Schüssel, Liz Mohn, Michael Spindelegger
(Foreign Minister of the Republic of Austria)

from left: Viviane Reding (Vice-President of the European
Commission), Jerome Zois, Ana Palacio (Foreign Minister of the
Kingdom of Spain)

Flowerbed in the Mirabelle Garden in front of the Mozarteum University

Nand Khemka (Chairman of the SUN Group),
Princess Jeet Nabha Khemka

Kurt Bock (CEO of BASF AG), Wilfried Haslauer (Governor of the State of Salzburg)

from left: Victor L. L. Chu (Chairman and CEO of the First Eastern Investment Group), Ida Tin (CEO and Co-Founder of Clue by BioWink), Henrietta Holsman Fore (Executive Director of UNICEF since 2018)

Angelika Vogel and Jürgen Strube (Honorary Chairman of the BASF
AG Supervisory Board)

from left: Initiators of the Trilogue Salzburg and Governor of the State
of Salzburg Wilfried Haslauer

2014

Ivan Mikloš (Former Finance Minister of the Slovak Republic)

Jörg Dräger (Member of the Bertelsmann Stiftung Executive Board)

from left: Sung-Joo Kim (Chairperson and CVO of the Sungjoo Group and MCM Holding AG), Brigitte Mohn (Member of the Bertelsmann Stiftung Executive Board), Henrietta Holsman Fore (Executive Director of UNICEF since 2018)

Veit Sorger (Former President of the Federation of Austrian Industries), Sung-Joo Kim (Chairperson and CVO of the Sungjoo Group and MCM Holding AG)

Kandeh K. Yumkella (UN Special Representative for Sustainable Energy for All)

Werner J. Bauer (Chairman of the Nestlé Deutschland AG Supervisory Board)

Jürgen Strube (Honorary Chairman of the BASF SE Supervisory Board)

Viviane Reding (Member of the European Parliament)

Wilfried Haslauer (Governor of the State of Salzburg), Benny Landa (Chairman and CEO of the Landa Group)

Video message from Edgar H. Schein (Professor Emeritus at the Sloan School, MIT), in the background from left: Dmitry Aksenov (Founder and Chairman of the RDI Group), Viviane Reding (Member of the European Parliament), Aart de Geus (Chairman of the Bertelsmann Stiftung Executive Board, 2012–2019), Harald Mahrer (State Secretary in the Austrian Ministry for Science, Research and Economics, 2014–2017), Lencke Steiner (Chairwoman of the trade association Die Jungen Unternehmer BJU)

from left: Eliezer Nechama (Director of the Bialik Rogozin School),
Liz Mohn, Rekha and Aaron Purie (Founder of the India Today Group)

Liz Mohn, Aart de Geus (Chairman of the Bertelsmann Stiftung)

Ian Goldin (Professor of Globalisation and Development at Oxford University)

Aaron Purie (Chairman and Editor-in-Chief at the India Today Group)

Eliezer Nechama (Director of the Bialik Rogozin School)

Marc Elsberg (Author)

Cardinal Reinhard Marx (Archbishop of Munich and Freising)

Yuki Tan (Chairwoman of Isthmus Pte Ltd.)

from left: Brigitta Pallauf (President of the Salzburg State Parliament), Wolfgang Schüssel, Liz Mohn

from left: Lulu Gurría, Angel Gurría (Secretary-General of the OECD), Liz Mohn, Princess Jeet Nabha Khemka, Brigitta Pallauf, Wolfgang Schüssel

from left: Peter Terium (former CEO of innogy SE), Tania Terium, Liz Mohn, Pascal Lamy (Former Director-General of the World Trade Organization)

from left: Victor L. L. Chu (Chairman and CEO of the First Eastern Investment Group), Irene Chu, Liz Mohn, Philipp Rösler (Former Vice-Chancellor of the Federal Republic of Germany)

Wolfgang Schüssel, Sarah Wedl-Wilson (Chairwoman of the
Supervisory Board of the Salzburg Easter Festival)

Ivan Krastev (Bulgarian political scientist)

Princess Jeet Nabha Khemka, Werner Bauer (Chairman of the
Bertelsmann Stiftung Board of Trustees)

Angel Gurría (Secretary-General of the OECD)

Harold James (Professor of History and International Politics at Princeton University)

Sarah Wedl-Wilson (Chairwoman of the Supervisory Board of the Salzburg Easter Festival)

from left: Liz Mohn, Wolfgang Schüssel, Ursula von der Leyen
(President of the European Commission)

Brigitte Bierlein (Federal Chancellor of Austria), Liz Mohn

Karin Schlautmann (Executive Vice-President of Corporate Communications at Bertelsmann SE), Markus Dohle (CEO of Penguin Random House)

Carsten Coesfeld (President of Telecommunications at Arvato Bertelsmann), Liz Mohn, Julia Gäckler

Elhadj As Sy (Secretary General of the International Federation of
Red Cross and Red Crescent Societies)

Carsten Coesfeld (President of Telecommunications at Arvato
Bertelsmann)

On the Future of the European Labor Market

Europe is a work in progress. Only through constant change can it grow together organically. That this work is still incomplete can be seen in how employment is developing and how the future labor market is being shaped. This is a crucial issue for Europe, since without jobs, without the prospect of finding work, people become unsettled and stressed.

The organic convergence of the labor market has been a key topic for the European Union since its founding. In addition to the free movement of goods and capital, as well as the freedom of establishment and the freedom to provide services, the free movement of workers has been a cornerstone of European integration. The basis for this was laid out in the Treaty of Rome: Unequal treatment was to be prevented and free choice of employment guaranteed. Efforts to promote mobility and regulate social security followed. Yet given the challenges it faces, Europe must continue to change if it wants to overcome the shortage of ideas, innovations and workers that has arisen globally, and if it intends to create new options for developing its own labor market.

Europe is a consensus and a commitment to rules and values – including on the labor market. Instead of recognizing these values as a European achievement and defining them as such, we still tend to attribute certain characteristics to citizens of specific countries: Germans are thorough, Italians fashionable, Finns adept at technology, Austrians environmentally conscious, etc. – and this, even though Europe's regulations are designed to codify exactly these European attributes as a generally applicable standard, including on the labor market. Basic rights, such as free movement, vocational training and worker protection, have now been established, and many people in Europe have benefitted from this. Moreover, it has permanently changed the situation in other countries. And that is something Europe can be proud of.

Nevertheless, conditions vary on the European job market, even beyond the structural differences. For example, when it comes to atypical employment, people in Germany tend to work part-time or have longer fixed-term contracts, while in countries like France, Italy and Finland, it is more common for people to have shorter fixed-term contracts or be running their own one-man or one-woman business. Standardizing the European labor market by using cross-border regulations and common social security systems could bring additional benefits. But would such steps even be possible, given that pressure already exists in various countries to reform social security systems on the national level? Ultimately, as the number of gainfully employed people declines, so do the contributions paid into social security programs. How then are these programs to be funded in the future?

The scope of the European labor market

One of the key successes of the European idea is that, for over 70 years, it has been possible to shape economic progress, social cohesion and framework conditions in a way that has generally been fair. This has also provided people with employment. The number of jobs that depend directly or indirectly on EU exports to countries outside of the European Union has risen continuously. While exports were responsible for 21.7 million jobs in 2000, by 2017 the figure had increased to 36 million. Each billion euros in EU exports provides some 13,000 people with employment. That shows the strength of Europe's export economy.

Global competition of this sort can also lead to job losses, although the European labor market has often been successful in overcoming new challenges. Even if other global regions have suffered more, Europe's labor market has often been hard hit by economic fluctuations, employment crises, different working conditions and high unemployment. Across the EU, 15.5 million people are currently without work. Greece and Spain are particularly affected here. This has consequences – especially for Europe's young people. What prospects can we offer them for a secure future? It is alarming when large segments of the younger population do not have work, when an entire generation might have little chance of a viable future and becomes completely discouraged as a result.

European Union and Eurozone: Youth Unemployment Rate, 2010–2020

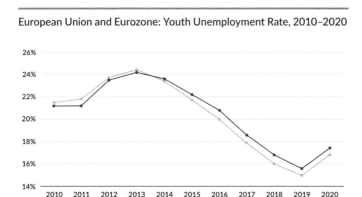

EU-27   Eurozone   Youth Unemployment Rate

Source: Eurostat; authors' calculations

At the same time, the European labor market is at a turning point – if for no other reason than the megatrends of globalization and digitalization. The impacts of these trends have never been as dramatic as they are today – including for Europe's labor market. They are transforming all our lives and the basic conditions under which we will work in the future.

Globalization is ensuring that businesses can expand old markets and enter new ones. Additionally, companies are becoming more and more diverse. Activities, production processes and value chains now stretch across national borders as a matter of course. In today's globalized world, it has long been outdated to think nationally and rely on individual strengths. Its sense of community and the diversity of its people are what make Europe strong. At the same time, however, countries have never been as dependent on each other, due to their trade relations. How, then, is the global economy changing society – and the way we work?

Even more striking are undoubtedly the changes arising from digitalization. We often forget that the single market is the strongest growth driver, but it has not yet gone digital. Digitalization is constantly giving rise to new conditions and making others obsolete. Neither its advancing pace nor the new possibilities it presents are foreseeable. New technologies are bringing the world closer together bit by bit. Our young talents think and act, live and work globally. The world has already become their workplace.

We must make greater use of the opportunities that digitalization offers in Europe, however. After all, the continent boasts prime conditions for realizing a digital single market. If we were faster in creating common rules, global champions could also emerge and create jobs here. Yet there are also risks: Because of digitalization, many of today's occupations will no longer exist in a few years' time. Perhaps not enough new jobs will be generated. People's fears of being replaced by machines and technology are not unfounded. We must alleviate their fears by giving them new hopes and opportunities for a brighter future.

The changing world of work will result in new types of jobs as well as erratic, heterogeneous work histories. At the same time, our social security systems are not yet designed to deal with new types of employment and recurring job changes, such as when people become freelancers after having been on a corporate payroll. Including people with disabilities in the European labor market is also a major challenge. In the EU, only half of all people with disabilities are gainfully employed, and of those less than 30 percent work full time. All too often, the potential that women have to offer remains untapped. In many European countries, they do better when obtaining educational degrees, and their social skills are needed more than ever. Nonetheless, they must still fight for recognition, for better working conditions and for better opportunities to balance their personal and professional lives. Current studies show that women are among those groups that have been particularly disadvantaged during the Covid-19 pandemic, since they are still the ones who do most of the household chores and look after children – which has a negative impact on their work-life balance and career development opportunities. Correspondingly, women in Europe are sorely under-represented not only in leadership positions, but also as founders of new businesses (depending on the country).

Perception of Change in Work-Life Balance and Career Development Opportunities, Comparison of Women and Men

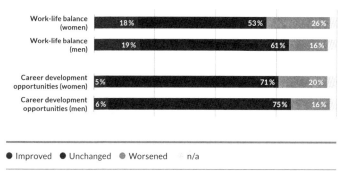

● Improved ● Unchanged ● Worsened   n/a

Source: Ipsos

Employment, productivity, innovation, sustainability, opportunities and economic growth all depend on the qualifications employees at existing companies have and which new businesses are launched. There is one problem, however, that will continue to grow in coming decades. Not only will there be a shortage of skilled workers in certain sectors, in Europe in particular there will be a mismatch between the supply of skills and the demand for them. Do we have the right qualifications to master current and coming challenges? Education and employment – they are the key to ensuring our societies have a viable future.

The danger of an aging population

All these challenges coincide with another change of global significance: For the first time in history, societies are getting older and the average age is increasing – a freely chosen development. Europe, where this trend is the most pronounced, will experience an orderly and controlled social stabilization as its population declines over the long term.

Projection of Working-age Population by Region

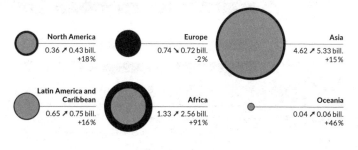

	North America	Europe	Asia
	0.36 ↗ 0.43 bill.	0.74 ↘ 0.72 bill.	4.62 ↗ 5.33 bill.
	+18%	-2%	+15%

Latin America and Caribbean
0.65 ↗ 0.75 bill.
+16%

Africa
1.33 ↗ 2.56 bill.
+91%

Oceania
0.04 ↗ 0.06 bill.
+46%

● 2020　● 2050

Source: Deutsche Stiftung Weltbevölkerung (2020). *DSW-Datenreport 2020*. Hannover. pp. 8–16.

Even though the most highly developed countries (especially in Europe) are bearing the brunt of demographic change – in the form of skilled labor shortages and shrinking and aging populations – this trend will gradually spread to the global level. How we respond to this development, in which labor and not capital is the decisive factor, will depend on two things above all: migration and occupational qualifications.

Migration and the competition for talent are already playing an increasingly important role. In the last decade, immigrants have accounted for most of the growth in the workforce in Europe and the US. Yet where are they supposed to come from in the future if more and more countries such as China also need well-trained workers? While Asia and Africa will be the regions where most of tomorrow's employees will be found, Europe faces the challenge of remaining attractive as a place to work. But what exactly will draw people to Europe in the future? And how can Europe find, develop and retain talented individuals for its labor market?

The answer to these questions could be: innovation and entrepreneurship, since they are playing a key role in positively shaping economic and social change in Europe. They are what could make it possible to attract and develop new talent. The international labor pool includes exceptionally well-trained young people, something that will remain true in the future. Yet young people are not the only ones who have something to offer within the European workforce. Other potential candidates include older, more experienced individuals who have already obtained a degree or qualification outside of Europe. The refugee crisis has shown how companies benefit when newcomers are integrated into the German and European labor market. In addition to rules, what we need if we want to ensure that things proceed fairly is better coordination between nations and

Migrants Living in Different Global Regions, by Region of Origin

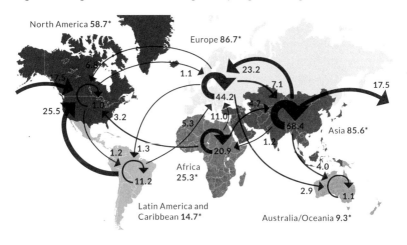

North America **58.7***

Europe **86.7***

6.6

7.5

1.1

23.2

7.1

17.5

25.5

1.0

3.2

44.2

11.0

4.7

68.4

Asia **85.6***

5.3

1.2

1.2

1.3

20.9

4.0

11.2

2.9

1.1

Africa **25.3***

Latin America and Caribbean **14.7***

Australia/Oceania **9.3***

*Total migration (2020, millions)   ↻ Migration from another country within the region
→ Migration from another global region

Source: https://www.un.org/development/desa/pd/content/international-migrant-stock; authors' calculations

businesses, so that talented workers can be deployed and promoted in the best possible manner.

The need for workers in certain sectors, such as banking, technology, media, telecommunications, nursing and health care, is only one aspect. Throughout the economy, it will be important to ensure people have both the skills that make them employable and opportunities for lifelong learning. After all, promoting education and knowledge across borders will remain our only possibility for making the world more social, just and peaceful. Both employers and employees must realize that workers will have to undergo further training and not merely remain in the same position with the same qualification. Options for education and training must therefore be developed that will allow workers to use their skills to become part of tomorrow's workforce.

The role of education and culture

Another question for the future will be: How can we help people cultivate their creativity? How can we put the framework in place that promotes entrepreneurship and gives people the freedom to create? This will be crucial if we want to continue competing globally over the long term. Given the challenges it faces, Europe will have to become a pioneer in addressing the global shortage of ideas, innovations and workers and finding ways to further develop its own labor market.

In the area of culture and science, the uniform European – and perhaps even global – labor market is often already a reality. Culture and art – in the form of architecture, painting, music and education – rarely stop at national borders, even if they are defined by regional or national influences. A Swedish architect plans office buildings in Paris, while a Polish violinist gives a concert in Vienna. Moreover, cooperative exchanges, international conferences and global knowledge networks create new possibilities for the future. The Erasmus program gives Europe's young people the opportunity for intercultural exchange – and to develop a European identity.

Thoughts, ideas and talents will be the most important economic drivers and thus providers of jobs. Brainpower will be the resource of the future. Europe will have to fight for its place in the global village – as a business location and way of life. The jobs young people take will no longer be located in their native country, but will extend beyond Europe to the entire world. That will increase the responsibility politicians, educators and employers have to join forces and actively support people in their professional development. Education is not a short sprint, it's a long-distance run in which the term "lifelong learning" is becoming ever more important.

Today, issues relating to employment are often addressed at the regional or national level. As the Trilogue Salzburg showed early on: Overcoming labor market challenges in Germany, Spain, Austria or Italy alone has not been possible for quite some time, which means the topic of employment must be approached from a European, if not an international perspective. The triad of culture, business and politics makes it possible to lay aside national vantage points, to regroup, to think ahead, to listen and to learn from each other – including when it comes to the future of the labor market.

Recommendations from Salzburg

The 2013 Trilogue Salzburg was dedicated to the topic "Competing for Talent: The Global Struggle for the World's Most Valuable Resource," and its discussions were informed by the realization that we will need more than 45 million additional workers by 2030 if the economy is to keep growing. In other words, in terms of new skilled workers, in less than 10 years Western Europe will have to add the equivalent of everyone employed in Germany, its largest economy. However, the pool from which qualified employees can be drawn is not infinite. The competition among companies, regions and countries will become tougher; at the same time, many countries are having difficulty removing the barriers preventing foreign workers from entering their labor market. The public is fully aware of the issues that await. Even in 2013, four out of five Germans assumed there would be too few qualified employees in coming decades and that Europe would have to become more attractive for skilled workers from abroad.

For that to happen, it will be necessary to increase mobility in a fundamental way. Back then, Viviane Reding, vice-president of the

European Commission from 2010 to 2014, gave a concise summary of the problem: "It's paradoxical: On the one hand, in Europe we have high unemployment rates while, on the other, there is a great need for well-trained workers." It's astonishing, she said, that there are basically no more borders for capital and trade flows, but the situation is completely different when it comes to labor mobility. As she explained, "We have a common market without borders and free movement of people. But mobility is not occurring the way we would like. People don't want to leave their comfort zone."

The Trilogue Salzburg has also shown that human capital will develop in coming years into one of the most valuable national resources and, simultaneously, that no location, company or country will be in a position to attract international talents on its own in the long run. Europe will have to take action and once again show its ongoing willingness to change – as a work in progress.

Even if other continents will also need skilled workers in the future, Europe is particularly affected here. It must therefore ensure that it remains attractive for skilled workers from Europe and abroad and that it supports the next generation of employees. Demetrios G. Papademetriou, president of the US-based Migration Policy Institute, said, "Immigration must be part of a broad social and economic policy strategy – one that encompasses education, training, employment, welfare, research and investment, and that goes well beyond the responsibilities of immigration authorities."

To be competitive, it is not enough to attract the best candidates and try to recruit people with scarce skills on the global job market. Investing in talent and promoting education at home and abroad are at least as important. Such measures ensure that the competition for talent does not devolve into a zero-sum game with winners and losers. Wolfgang Aulitzky, a professor at Cornell University who is originally from Austria, warned back then that the immigration of highly qualified workers results in a brain gain for Europe or the US, but the brain drain in the migrants' native countries can lead to major problems – "especially if there is a shortage of doctors or nurses."

An expansion of the global talent pool can create benefits for everyone. However, better coordination between nations and companies is needed to ensure that employees are deployed and developed

in the best possible way. The public and private sectors must coop-
erate more closely if they are to meet the changing requirements.

The expectations directed towards Europe's neighborhood for
solving this problem are clear. Participants at the Trilogue recognized
the considerable potential Asia and Africa have as a source of skilled
workers. It was therefore apparent even back then that Europe must
become attractive to workers on the national and international
levels, if it wants to take the necessary steps, such as promoting
young talent, and thereby ensure that the European labor market
remains stable over time. After all, other regions – Asia and America
in particular – also require skilled workers. Overall, however, more
and diverse solutions are needed on the global, national and corporate level:

- Data collection should be improved on the global level so that
  the necessary comparisons can be made. The latter can help
  track the factors driving mobility and identify how skilled
  workers are moving internationally. That would allow policy
  makers and business leaders to make better decisions based on
  empiric data. Other recommendations developed by the Trilogue
  participants include holding an annual European "talent summit"
  and tying international trade agreements to migration-related
  issues. That would promote a more intensive exchange of experience on the international level.
- Migration policy must be evaluated and suitable assistance
  programs for migrants created to support the mobility of skilled
  workers on the national level. Unnecessary obstacles could thus
  be removed and the attractiveness of individual destination
  countries increased. With that, Europe could become a role
  model for other countries. In addition to clear and fair rules for
  immigration, what is important here is having suitable regulations
  for acquiring citizenship, recognizing qualifications and allowing immigrants' families to join them at a later date.
- Austria, Germany and Switzerland urgently need talented individuals and solutions for their aging societies. Joint strategies
  should be developed, given the countries' shared language and
  similar economic structures. Language education could become
  one component in a qualification package used in selected sectors,

thereby turning it into a collective advantage for all three German-speaking nations.

- The employment of women is a key factor in the search for talent, since they represent half of the available human capital. It is therefore crucial that women be included more in the workforce and that greater effort be made to promote their advancement. In societies that do not achieve this, over half the knowledge they have at their disposal will remain untapped, which will then impact societal productivity.
- Especially those places with existing concentrations of human capital must become attractive to new skilled workers. That is what allows certain locations to become innovation and talent hubs, which have a positive influence on the surrounding cities and regions, giving rise to innovations. Silicon Valley is a prime example of how the arrival of talent and companies can improve the economic situation for an entire region.

Thoughts on Innovation and Education

Viviane Reding
Former Vice-President of the European Commission and
European Commissioner for Justice, Fundamental Rights
and Citizenship

Europe's businesses are already facing a significant lack of personnel, which will worsen in the years to come. How can we attract additional workers?

> *There is plenty of talent. But it is often wasted – for various reasons: because it remains unutilized (the female gap) or unchanneled (we need to develop a general culture for technological knowledge). And we should instill enthusiasm for our European project, so that young talents feel the need to be part of it!*

How can we foster risk-taking and entrepreneurship and, as a result, innovation?

> *There certainly is a risk-taking gap in Europe. Although things have become better at the early-stage level (thanks to the entrepreneurship of the young start-up community), there is still a VC gap at the mature level. The massive investment programs the EU has launched lately could and should help if they are channeled into venture and not into subsidies.*

20 years of the Trilogue Salzburg: What was your "Trilogue moment"?

20 years of a one-of-its-kind Trilogue. The astonishing mixture of character, experience, diversity, wisdom. Friends from around the world look forward every year to sharing ideas in a place of beauty and history. For me, personally, the Trilogue is a gift. A lifelong-learning experience with never-ending highlights. Thank you for this treasure!

Challenges for Modern Leadership

The megatrends of globalization, digitalization and demographic change are defining the challenges that political and business leaders will face in the future. Each of these developments puts leaders and cultures to the test, in both everyday business settings and the political sphere. Yet this is not only true for leaders; employees and ordinary citizens are also experiencing these changes and expect solutions from decision makers.

These megatrends are changing the working world, business models and organizational structures. On the one hand, leaders are still responsible for achieving success in increasingly competitive global markets; on the other, they must demonstrate responsibility on an ongoing basis by treating those they lead with respect. First and foremost, this means having a flexible leadership style that matches the current situation, task and circumstances and yet does justice to the relevant values and standards.

Digitalization in particular is having far-reaching consequences for today's leaders. Since data can be captured and evaluated faster and more quickly than ever before, sounder decisions can be made. The difficulty lies less in ensuring the necessary openness and transparency – after all, leaders themselves are becoming more visible. Their personal lives and their decisions can be observed, critiqued and condemned at almost every opportunity. But does that make a leader's thoughts, doubts and concerns more transparent?

The members of Generation Z – those born between 1995 and 2010 – are questioning everything: themselves, but also the environment in which they live and work. They are demanding to participate and, as they do, they bring the skills with them that ensure companies succeed in these digital times. They are often searching for a purpose – a why and wherefore. Thanks to the generation that lives and thinks digitally, the world is being transformed – as is leadership. This is especially true in those places where people are working from home, separated physically but connected virtually. Yet can we already foresee how these new forms of work will change our collaborations and cultures, especially at businesses? No technology will replace face-to-face encounters anytime soon, since they make it possible to convey much more than just words and images.

Social changes also pose new challenges for leaders. Rarely have employees been able to realize their individual potential and shape their own lives as much as they can today. As a result, rarely have leaders been so called upon to meet the interests of society or their organization, and to fulfill the individual wishes of their employees.

Growing doubts among executives

A representative survey carried out by the Bertelsmann Stiftung of nearly 1,000 executives in Germany shows that 30 percent of the respondents experience a high level of stress as leaders. Asked to respond using a standard scale, one in five (21.4%) said they cannot meet their own standards, since not only must they fulfill others' expectations, they must also take a changing society into account, as that is the environment in which they are supposed to act effectively.

Leadership has never been easy, even in less challenging times. Those who lead can make the wrong decision and reap criticism as a result. The performance of political leaders is especially prone to scrutiny. Public opinion is anything but positive: People feel decisions take too long, there is a lack of vision, compromises are inadequate. This is reflected in the oft-bemoaned loss of trust in government and political leaders.

Business leaders have received less than top marks since the financial and banking crisis at the latest. The sector is decried for various irresponsible activities such as commercial and balance-sheet fraud, not to mention overwhelmed executives, inadequate crisis management, and too few women in high-level positions. There has also been a considerable loss of trust in the economic elite, even if it may not be as pronounced as in other fields. Scientists and researchers are often the only ones people say they trust.

Varying Trust in Societal Leaders and Specific Groups

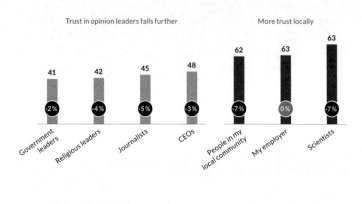

Trust in opinion leaders falls further   More trust locally

Source: Edelman Trust Barometer 2021: p. 19. https://www.edelman.com/sites/g/files/aatuss191/files/2021-01/2021-edelman-trust-barometer.pdf

Anyone who assumes responsibility for people must earn their trust – whether in politics, culture or business. This is not always easy: Leadership means being a role model. We need role models in all parts of society once again, above all in politics and business. Sharing values and treating each other with respect are the basis for social harmony – in both professional and political settings. In addition, however, leaders must always critically question their own actions: Am I doing the right thing? Is there a better way?

As business and political leaders well know, the decisions they must make are rarely based on clear, unequivocal information. Leadership is always accompanied by uncertainty. Leaders in a position of responsibility have their doubts, including about themselves. But that is precisely the hallmark of good leadership: the courage to make decisions even when there is concern or skepticism, when there is no absolute clarity and not everyone agrees. After all, in neither politics nor business is there ever absolute clarity about what tomorrow will bring – yet assistance and guidance are needed exactly when things are unclear. That is when leaders need their own role models to help them find their way. Mentors are therefore essential, since they provide support and give advice when difficult decisions loom.

Even without such decision-making pressure, leaders need motivating, supportive conditions if they are to lead effectively, promote creativity and innovation in their teams, and implement change. What increases the motivation and commitment of everyone involved are dialogue-driven interactions and clear communication. Also required, however, are basic values that leaders can use for guidance. This is where mentors again play an important role, since effective role models are the ones who help instill values.

Openness and transparency, courage and creativity, solidarity and goodwill are important cornerstones in this regard. Yet qualities such as discipline and responsibility, as well as self-initiative and freedom, are necessary for strengthening and anchoring the framework conditions. Creating such a culture is a prerequisite for modern leadership. In the business world, this is the key task that senior executives, supervisory boards and shareholders all face. In the political sphere, it's about shaping the future of the democracy we want to live in.

One task that leaders continue to face is moving people along the path of change. People have always sought stability, security, purpose, continuity and values, and rightly so. Leaders must develop visions and set goals that can make this possible. Many people today seem to firmly agree with the statement once made by Germany's former chancellor, Helmut Schmidt: "Anyone who has visions should consult a doctor." Yet leadership cannot succeed without goals.

Sometimes people think leaders should meet the demands made of them all at once. They want visions that can substitute for prophesies – knowing what tomorrow will bring as if seen in a crystal ball. What gets forgotten here is that leaders are also ordinary human beings, neither all knowing nor all powerful. Everyone is aware of what happened 10 years ago, but no one can say with certainty what will occur 10 days from now. Visions can and should be developed and communicated, albeit primarily to realize the goals and tasks they imply, and not to still the need for purported security.

How leaders are seen

Yet what actually makes someone a leader? What is needed for a person to develop leadership qualities? The list of desirable traits fills countless books. Even if some manuals seem to make it easy for leaders – leadership cannot be taken for granted. And every leader has his or her own style. A centralistic and hierarchical style generally no longer meets today's requirements. The desire to have an open, understanding and charismatic person in charge – often understood as "leadership" – and the need for that person to monitor, steer and take decisive action – often referred to as "management" – are not always easily reconcilable. Ultimately, each individual must decide which leadership style is suitable for his or her own personality, for the current situation and for the existing system of values. Recognizing this is a leader's job.

From the middle of the 19th century until the 1930s, the belief existed that some people are born leaders and have a right to lead – monarchies are a good example. During the 1940s, these beliefs about "great men" or "great women" expanded to include innate qualities that each person has, thereby enlarging the circle of what had hitherto been a very exclusive group of leaders (trait theories). Anyone who was intelligent, empathetic and creative was seen as a good leader.

While the theories of the 1950s focused on the behavior and actions of leaders (behavioral theories), the context and situation in which the leadership occurred was seen as the deciding factor in the 1960s (contingency theories). The theories of the 1970s, in contrast, examined the relationship between leaders and followers, seeing effective leadership as the balance between reward and punishment (transactional theories). The theories that emerged in the 1980s began featuring the word "trust." Intrinsic motivation arising from the trust between leader and follower was now seen as the driving force (transformational theories).

Evolution of Leadership Theory

Trait Theories
Carlyle: "Great Man" Theory
Max Weber: Charisma Theory

Behavioral Theories
Max Weber: Leadership Styles
Lewin/Lippitt/White: Iowa Styles
Fleishman: Ohio State Leadership Quadrant
Tannenbaum/Schmidt: Leadership Continuum
Blake/Mouton: Behavioral Grid

Situational Theories
Fiedler: Contingency Model
Hersey/Blanchard: Maturity Model
House: Path-Goal Theory
Vroom/Yetton: Situational Decision Model

Transformational Theories
House: Neo-charismatic Leadership
Bass: Transformational Leadership
Manz/Sims: Leadership through Self-Leadership
Bass/Steidlmeier: Authentic Leadership
Pearce/Sims: Shared Leadership

Systemic Leadership

| 1841 | 1921 | 1939 | 1953 | 1964 | 1969 | 1971 | 1977 | 1985 | 1991 | 1999 | 2006 | 2016 |
| 1922 | | | 1950 | 1967 | | 1973 | | | | 2000 | | |

Source: Authors' depiction

In sum, the leadership theories highlighted a series of new contextual factors in order to explain effective or successful leadership. Nonetheless, the basic definition of leadership remained the same: a process for achieving a goal.

Individuals need solid training and valid, specialized knowledge if they are to hold exceptional positions. Politics is an area in which we need many more people who meet that description. Even if numerous consultants are available to ensure decisions are soundly made, expertise cannot always be gained cheaply or quickly. And it would be better if leaders had this expert knowledge themselves. One thing that cannot be allowed, moreover, is that large amounts of money are spent on consulting services and the decisions reached are unacceptable nevertheless.

In the past, knowledge was passed on through stories, books and shared experiences. Until the middle of the last century, leaders – whose role, at least in business, was much influenced by industrialization – were largely known for their ability to plan, steer, budget, organize and solve problems. They were responsible for these tasks and ensured everything went smoothly and efficiently. Their knowledge was thus applied to their operational activities and could easily be passed along to others. Even today, legions of instructors at schools, universities and businesses are employed to impart this knowledge. Yet is that enough to overcome the challenges confronting political and business leaders?

Endangered Corporate Culture

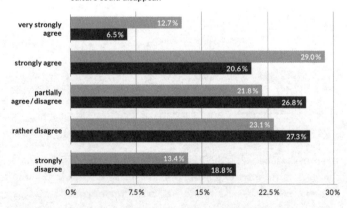

When my staff are working from home, I feel that our corporate culture could disappear.

	2021	2020
very strongly agree	12.7%	6.5%
strongly agree	29.0%	20.6%
partially agree/disagree	21.8%	26.8%
rather disagree	23.1%	27.3%
strongly disagree	13.4%	18.8%

● 2021 ● 2020

Source: Bertelsmann Stiftung (forthcoming). *Führungskräfte-Radar 2021*. Gütersloh.

Being a specialist or expert does not mean one can ignore one's intuition, which is arguably one of the most important qualities for leaders today. Anyone who wants to make a difference in society must leave the beaten path – must be ready to rethink conventional wisdom and be curious about the new. Those who go beyond previously explored territory can develop many new ideas and attitudes. This is another thing that is characteristic of today's leaders: They are creative and can think outside the box to solve problems in new ways.

The development of new organizational concepts, such as servant leadership or holacracy, and the calls for ever flatter hierarchies, or even their abolition, clearly show that leadership itself – and the justification for having people serve as leaders – is being questioned more than ever. Yet who would make the decisions and assume responsibility if there were no more leaders?

New leadership prototype needed?

Given all this, many leaders are asking themselves new, substantive questions: What will leadership look like in the future? How much flexibility can I make possible? How open am I really when I interact with employees? How much courage do I have to try something new? Which values are important to me, and how can they guide me in creating modern career paths that take the individual and the interests of my organization into account in equal measure? How can the quality of leadership be improved in the business world and, above all, in the political sphere? How can innovative thinkers – and not just defenders of the status quo – be moved into leadership positions?

Participants in the 2015 Trilogue Salzburg looked at exactly those questions. From August 5 to 7, political, economic and cultural representatives came together once again to discuss the lack of leadership in politics and business and its implications, in keeping with the event's motto: "In Search of Leadership – A Critical Requirement for Governance, Social Cohesion and Competitiveness?" The gathering also focused on the qualities and capabilities that individuals in politics and business need in order to be considered for leadership positions in the 21st century.

The need to discuss leadership and responsibility becomes even more apparent when we consider the consequences of the actions taken by leaders. After all, leadership does not occur in a vacuum, but has an impact on society as well. With that, leadership takes on a new dimension: the leader's responsibility for society – since leadership means assuming responsibility not only for oneself and those in one's immediate environment, but also for the weaker members of society and for society as a whole.

The co-originator of organizational psychology, Ed Schein of the United States, showed that growing technological complexity and speed, increased networking and multiculturalism, and the linking of economic goals, sustainability and social responsibility would significantly complicate leadership in the future – a trend that will surely continue.

As the experiences of the Trilogue's participants showed, decisions about how to solve coming problems are often made by only a few people. In this situation, leaders cannot promise more than they can deliver, such as gifts to voters or employees. Instead, the focus must be on goals and values that can be attained.

A vision can serve as a compass here. To that end, it is necessary to strengthen leadership in the political, business and cultural contexts. The discussions at the Trilogue also showed that leadership in business and politics has many similarities with leadership in the cultural sphere. A good leader has to like people and trust them. The conductor Franz Welser-Möst noted that, when he was leading the Cleveland Orchestra, the speeches he had to give and the visions and concepts he had to convey were much different than those of his predecessors. A critical point for him was that "leaders shape and change, managers manage. In other words, they administer." He did not want soldiers or robots in his orchestra, he said, but creative musicians. As the gathering in Salzburg showed yet again: Business, culture and politics can learn from each other much more frequently than they do.

Back then, Wilfried Haslauer, governor of the state of Salzburg, noted the changes affecting leadership culture, which was, he said, becoming more reserved, polite and empathetic. According to Lencke Wischhusen, then national chairwoman of the Junge Unternehmer trade association, even if a patriarchal style of leadership no longer prevails in many places but has given way to teamwork and communication, at the end of the day a firm hand is needed.

As the discussions in Salzburg have made clear, leading in a complex world means rethinking the requirements needed to be a leader. Moreover, the search for good leadership is more than an academic question – it means examining the value ascribed to leadership itself. At the same time, the Trilogue showed that the desire for charismatic leaders remains controversial. This desire will persist in the future, the participants agreed, yet things can get explosive when it comes to populist figures, if their charisma is not guided by a moral compass. Referring to this problem, BASF Supervisory Board Chairman Jürgen Strube said, "The most charismatic leaders of the 20th century were Hitler, Stalin and Mao. We know where that led."

Leadership – as the participants knew from practical experience – means taking risks. Former European Commissioner Viviane Reding noted that in a society fixated on security, everyone defends their own position and no one moves forward. "Since today's generation grew up in considerable security, it shies away from risks, challenges and entrepreneurship," she said. That is why there are more managers than true leaders, she pointed out, alluding to the remarks by Welser-Möst. "When there are problems, we in Europe respond with new rules, not new ideas."

The key findings and recommendations from Salzburg remain just as valid today as they were then:

- Education in particular should be used to create a culture and attitudes that impart leadership and cultural sensitivity – leadership can be taught and learned.
- Leadership is not a topic for the elite – every individual can be a leader in his or her field.
- Leadership requires role models – ambassadors of successful leadership are needed.
- Leadership means taking responsibility and risks. Society is promoting both to an insufficient degree.
- The diversity of people, values, cultures and mentalities requires leaders with a high level of competence.

- The privacy of leaders must also be protected.
- A modern approach to leadership needs new systems of incentives when it comes to compensation, benefits, etc., but also in terms of access to elites, power, etc.
- Young leaders need support on their developmental path.

Educating leaders is thus of critical importance if challenges are to be overcome. In addition to the business sphere, we need professionalized framework conditions in the political arena for teaching and learning leadership.

Thoughts on the Challenges of Modern Leadership

Marc Elsberg
Bestselling Author

What are the elements of leadership today?

- *Walking the talk (see Question 3)*
- *Thinking in a way that is long-term, networked, global and cognizant of society as a whole*
- *Finding solutions for the challenges of our time – climate crisis, human rights, threats to democracy and rule of law – instead of explanations aka excuses, or spinning things to say why it's all "not so easy" or a "climate, eco, social dictatorship," etc.*

Which values are fundamental for sustainable leadership?

- *Human rights*
- *True humility instead of hubris – a leader is no one without other people*
- *Cooperation instead of egotism and ruthless competition*

How can we re-establish trust in democracy, politics and business? Why has trust in institutions eroded and how dangerous is that erosion?

"Walk the talk." Trust in institutions has declined primarily because, for ideological reasons, government institutions have increasingly been deprived of expertise and funding in recent decades and, with them, the opportunity to shape things. Most of the private (and

increasingly political) elites (leading managers and politicians, etc.) have, however, used this freedom only to enrich themselves at society's expense instead of living up to their responsibility – their favorite argument for their often obscenely high compensation (especially in the private sector) – and improving things for society as a whole.

Institutions are barely able or willing to do anything to prevent this now-structuralized plundering of society by the "elites," or their representatives are increasingly participating in it themselves.

Nor do they promote the values that the West has pledged itself to, namely human rights, so they can make what are literally murderous deals with dictators instead. The institutional representatives have become compliant henchmen of the dealmakers, who have spent decades preventing the implementation of the needed policy measures (effective climate protection, proper supply chain laws, respect for human rights, etc.). This "transformation through trade" (irony alert!) has long since changed the West more for the worse than its trading partners for the better.

The loss of trust will only be reversed when these "elites" stop being hypocritical and start setting an example by actually living the values they are constantly invoking.

20 years of the Trilogue Salzburg: What was your "Trilogue moment"?

There was not just one moment for me, but many small, human moments during private conversations between events or in the evenings, which did more to promote mutual understanding than the discussion about the major issues.

Values, Responsibility and Social Cohesion

The world's fragmentation is becoming more pronounced and tangible, something we are also experiencing in the area of social values. The rapidly progressing developments taking place on our globe are unsettling many people and making them afraid of what the future might bring. More and more people are becoming susceptible to intolerance, populism and even hatred.

We know that people want security. Yet we also know that we must learn to deal with impending challenges. When it comes to what social cohesion will be like in the future, two questions are important:

- What gives people guidance and stability?
- What connects people with each other?

Different cultures, languages, religions and traditions have become everyday realities. This diversity enriches our lives and offers numerous opportunities. Not only do different perspectives, experiences and approaches make it possible to try new paths, they give rise to new ideas. It is important to acknowledge that coming into contact with other people can often be a very inspiring, valuable experience. Yet living in cultural diversity can itself be a challenge, one that must be actively managed. Fear of the new or unknown can lead people to oppose more diversity and change.

A key question will be how to deal with the conflicts that arise from the multiplicity of values found in rapidly changing societies. To that end, neither extreme homogeneity and conformity, on the one hand, nor heterogeneity and individualism, on the other, will ensure social cohesion in the future.

Social harmony depends on our finding an effective way to respond to diversity. Society faces the considerable task of forming a social whole from the dynamic interplay of different values, life goals, heritages, religions and desires, a whole that guarantees solidarity, trust and freedom. For this to happen, it will be necessary to define exactly which diversity we are referring to.

Guiding values

Values offer guidance for life in society. They serve as a compass we can use to direct our actions. We often need such a compass to point the way in a world that is growing ever more complex. Shared values such as tolerance, freedom, solidarity, equal opportunity and goodwill are essential, especially when a society grows more diverse. They give people an identity and security. They give them a sense of belonging and allow them to feel at home. If we want to live together peacefully, we once again need a shared understanding of values.

Values form the foundation for social harmony on which everything else can be built. This solid foundation is the only thing that offers people the opportunity to develop, experience freedom and find fulfillment. Trust plays a decisive role here. People must be able to experiment, to take risks. These days, young people must take the initiative and shape their lives themselves, more so than in the past. They have to orient themselves and find their way among many different lifestyles and possibilities.

Bridges of understanding

What holds society together and connects us as people? Diversity is enriching but, as noted, it can be a source of tension. In a society in which people have different values, talking about those values is important. That is the only way to accept and understand each other, provide guidance, work together to promote social harmony, and overcome misunderstandings and conflicts.

Essentially, this means listening to and learning from one another. People need to know about other religions, cultures and values so they can understand each other better. Therefore, diversity must be more than merely tolerated. It must be acknowledged and actively shaped. At the same time, it is important that other cultures not be uprooted. In a global world, we must learn to live with each other instead of against each other.

Values such as trust and goodwill, openness and tolerance, responsibility and community are what hold societies together and create bridges of understanding across languages and borders. People of different cultures build these bridges by approaching and getting to know each other. That is the only way trust can grow – as a basis for living together successfully in diversity.

In the penultimate study carried out by the Bertelsmann Stiftung in 2017, three-quarters of Germans said they feel social cohesion in the country is at least partially at risk (37 % agreed, 36 % partially agreed). And even though the most recent study from 2020 shows that the values for social cohesion in Germany remain stable and high, a number of risks are still apparent. Declining prosperity, increasing unemployment and growing income inequality correlate with less cohesion – when compared across Germany's states and across different nations.

In the three years between the two studies, the overall index for social cohesion in Germany changed only minimally: In 2017, the combined index value was 60 points on a scale of 0 to 100 following recalculation; in 2020, it was slightly higher, at 61 points.

The study from 2020 also showed, however, that trust in political parties, in the federal government and in the national parliament declined noticeably in the intervening three years.

Connecting people, building bridges across languages and borders, promoting mutual understanding among peoples, cultures and religions – that will be the main task if social cohesion is to be strengthened now and in the future.

These efforts cannot stop at borders, however. A crucial aspect will be making connections across national borders, while also building bridges and promoting understanding – through encounters with representatives of all areas of society from both inside and outside Europe.

Social Cohesion

Overall, social cohesion in Germany is high and stable

2020 2017

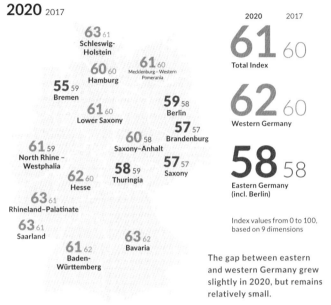

	2020	2017
Total Index	**61**	60
Western Germany	**62**	60
Eastern Germany (incl. Berlin)	**58**	58

Index values from 0 to 100, based on 9 dimensions

The gap between eastern and western Germany grew slightly in 2020, but remains relatively small.

Schleswig-Holstein **63** 61
Hamburg **60** 60
Mecklenburg – Western Pomerania **61** 60
Bremen **55** 59
Lower Saxony **61** 60
Berlin **59** 58
Brandenburg **57** 57
North Rhine – Westphalia **61** 59
Saxony–Anhalt **60** 58
Hesse **62** 60
Thuringia **58** 59
Saxony **57** 57
Rhineland–Palatinate **63** 61
Saarland **63** 61
Baden-Württemberg **61** 62
Bavaria **63** 62

Perceived cohesion (index): ● low (50 – <60) ● moderate (60 – <70)

Source: Authors' depiction

Reviving international cooperation and strengthening global alliances are therefore especially important. Many problems affect people in Gütersloh and Vienna just as they do people in Delhi, Istanbul, São Paolo, Moscow and Beijing. The goal must be to trustingly shape relations between peoples and cultures. To do this, we once again need visions of a shared future for our world, one in which people live together in peace.

Misguided by dogma

These visions require open-mindedness. We must courageously confront dogmatism and fundamentalism. No one can lay claim to the incontrovertible truth. After all, the truth is more controversial and contested today than ever before. Social networks in particular offer a platform for disseminating news and viewpoints to the entire world in a matter of seconds. Even the most outlandish opinions are suddenly visible to everyone, and the quality and validity of the statements made often recede into the background. Impediments to mutual understanding grow – and sometimes become insurmountable.

Fake news and "alternative facts" undermine trust and pose a threat to our shared existence. The consequences for our societies are serious. In a survey conducted by the Bertelsmann Stiftung for the Trilogue Salzburg, eight out of ten respondents in Germany and Austria said they had difficulty differentiating correct from false information. At the same time, more and more people are becoming isolated and withdrawing into the virtual world. Our societies are increasingly made up of loners.

Yet no society can survive without a sense of community. Now more than ever, we need an exchange of arguments and viewpoints. People must be able to come together and get to know each other. That means they have to interact openly, without prejudice. That is why, instead of dogmas, we need objective, fact-based dialogue.

Democracy as a foundation

But what will hold society together in the years to come? One answer is surely: to further develop democracy as a prerequisite for our shared future. That is what will ensure our freedom.

Freedom and democracy, however, are increasingly coming under fire in the Western world. Attacks from within and without are proliferating. We must therefore continue to develop democracy, so that it is more diverse, more up to date and, as a result, more sustainable.

Democracy thrives when people can get involved. It thrives when it is home to democrats! It needs people who are willing to pitch in.

If people can get involved and make a difference, if they sense that they have the freedom to act, then they will learn to appreciate the true value of democracy once again.

At the same time, we must not take democracy for granted. The risk would be too great in these challenging times. In Germany, Europe and around the world, people need a solid sense of trust and cohesion on the international level. But even in Europe, there is sometimes too little common understanding of Europe's own values and how they should be interpreted. The current discussions about discrimination, homophobia, vaccines, conspiracy theories, fake news and sustainability vividly demonstrate this. Thus, the social cohesion of our pluralistic societies is increasingly called into question. And even if the political mainstream is currently showing itself to be adaptive and robust against the temptations of populism, the threat of radicalization is growing.

How populist are Germans?

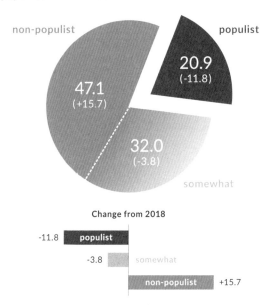

Percentage of all respondents; change from November 2018 in parenthesis.
Population sample: Germans 18 years or older (10,055 respondents in 2020).

Source: infratest dimap and YouGov on behalf of the Bertelsmann Stiftung

Effective politics in democracies thrives on patient negotiations and the painstaking search for compromises – on the art of aligning long-term visions with today's exigencies. Yet parts of the population no longer feel sufficiently represented and understood by politicians. People's doubts are growing, while questions are being raised about whether politics is effective at all. The disenchantment with politics is often seen at election time. A certain indifference towards politics is becoming evident in purportedly progressive Western countries in particular – and this despite the fact that, or because, prosperity has increased.

After all, the global rise in prosperity brought about by globalization has not only produced winners. As we have seen in recent years, for exactly that reason people who feel their prosperity is threatened are turning away from democracy.

Values in a digital world

As the Covid-19 pandemic has recently shown, our exchanges with each other in the digital age largely take place as discussions on computer screens. The anonymity of the Internet reduces inhibitions and facilitates discrimination and hostility more than in the past. Not only can that put a strain on social cohesion, it can destroy lives. That's why we need a new ethics and international laws as a foundation for our digital future.

Yet we have also seen that no technology can completely replace face-to-face interactions. After all, technological advances, such as artificial intelligence and the algorithms that analyze and influence human behavior, continue to put social cohesion to the test. We are experiencing the increasing impact that social networks and search engines are having, but are not always aware of how these technologies work, not to mention the far-reaching consequences they can have for society. It is still not completely clear how these technologies have influenced political events, such as the presidential election in the US and Britain's decision to leave the European Union. What is clear, however, is that the discourse on how to shape the digital world has just begun.

These essential ethical issues have implications for every citizen in society. Evaluating algorithms, processes and their outcomes might not always be easy in a complex world, but ultimately it is up to us to take action. That's because, even in a digital world, the crucial questions remain of how we want to live together as a society and which values are worth striving for.

Values education as a foundation

We need values education if we are to find our way in this dynamic world with its growing diversity and increasing challenges. Values education promotes the recognition of basic values while strengthening the ability to engage constructively with a range of values. It includes coming to terms with diverging values and deciding how one is going to orient oneself on an individual level. This also means accepting that other people have their own values – not only society's newcomers, but also those who already live here.

In the past, values were usually instilled in schools and community groups, during childhood by one's parents, and through religion, usually the one practiced by one's family.

However, the role played by parents, schools, community groups, civic organizations and religions has grown less important. Correspondingly, numerous factors exist that influence social cohesion. At the same time, social media now play a bigger role in instilling values. The risk is growing that people will become distrustful, uncertain and disoriented. Yet how can a fact-based dialogue take place in a filter bubble? It is therefore important that we find a peaceful language that promotes understanding, and that we view the world and its various cultures holistically.

Culture as a bridge-builder

Culture's creative power can increase understanding. This is something we clearly sense with music. The world is home to many cultures, yet we have only one common language: music. Music knows no borders. Music immediately touches the heart and soul.

Factors Influencing Social Cohesion

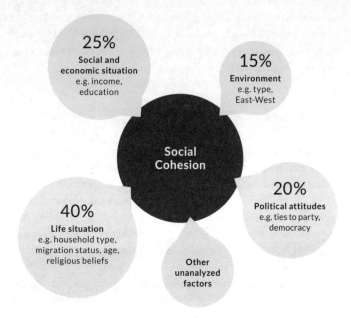

Simplified depiction of the results of a multivariable regression (in which explanatory factors = 100), with beta coefficients used as the basis for percentages

Source: Bertelsmann Stiftung / infas Institut für angewandte Sozialwissenschaft GmbH

It promotes tolerance and community and brings people of different nationalities, languages, religions and viewpoints together.

Music can generate a sense of community, which in turn leads to elementary communal experiences. Imagination, creativity and performance play a key role here. If music and singing were no longer taught, we would lose an important part of our culture, since they promote tolerance and international understanding.

Culture strengthens social participation, tolerance, respect and the ability to work as a team, while fostering self-development and social skills. Cultural exchange has an enormously stabilizing effect as a result. It is and will remain one way to promote peace.

Culture helps build bridges in another way: Numerous artists experience in their own lives the tension and conflict that arise between established tradition, current challenges and the need for public acceptance. Their unique, individual responses to this situation allow them to undergo a remarkable journey of self-development. They can thus be seen as ambassadors of tolerance, since they are in the constant process of striking a balance between identity and difference.

Trilogue Salzburg and social cohesion

The Trilogue Salzburg tries to build exactly such bridges for the future. The interactions with people from different countries and cultures, and the different perspectives on culture, business and politics provide inspiration, insight and encouragement all at the same time. Thanks to its lively discussions about values and principles, through the years the Trilogue Salzburg has also regularly examined the question of social cohesion.

The importance for Europe of common values and mutual understanding was addressed at the Trilogue as early as 2004, when the gathering examined the topic "A Modern Concept of Tolerance for Europe." A range of subjects dominated the public debate back then, such as headscarves, anti-Semitism in Europe, discrimination and terrorism.

The year 2004 was also decisive for Europe: The European Union gained 10 new members. For the community to expand, it was necessary to resolve conflicts, identify commonalities and communicate across existing differences.

The background paper prepared for the Trilogue that year was based on the latest research and fundamentally informed by UNESCO's 1995 Declaration of the Principles of Tolerance: "Tolerance is respect, acceptance and appreciation of the rich diversity of our world's cultures, our forms of expression and ways of being human. It is fostered by knowledge, openness, communication, and freedom of thought, conscience and belief. Tolerance is harmony in difference. It is not only a moral duty, it is also a political and legal requirement. Tolerance, the virtue that makes peace possible, contributes to the replacement of the culture of war by a culture of peace."

Director Andrea Breth pointed out at the start that tolerance costs a lot. How willing is a society, she asked, to accept the virtually infinite list of problems, like the wars and conflicts in former Yugoslavia and in Sudan, as well as increasing unemployment and the lack of medicine for AIDS patients in Africa, not to mention the greed of consumers, who want things to be "as cheap as possible." In art, tolerance is a given, said singer Helen Donath, since singing together unites people.

More tolerance would also help in politics, the participants agreed back then, noting that the key question for diverse, heterogeneous societies is how to achieve social consensus without necessarily having a common understanding of values. This is also a challenge for Europe, where there is no shared understanding of what tolerance is or where it begins and ends, they said, something that is increasingly posing a challenge to social cohesion in our pluralistic societies. According to the participants, tolerance is becoming more and more important in resolving ethnic, religious, cultural and gender-related conflicts. What is needed, they said, is a sustainable model of tolerance that presupposes the proactive engagement of all societal forces so they can continually renegotiate how differences are addressed.

Jürgen Strube, then chairman of the BASF Supervisory Board, stressed the importance of tolerance for business enterprises. In the private sector, he said, efforts are being made to combine the best values from several countries and introduce them into corporate culture. "I believe that for transnational corporations as well as for the leading economic players around the world, tolerance is not only a must – for most it is already a fact of life," he explained.

From today's perspective, the words of the Irish lawyer, politician and manager Peter D. Sutherland, almost sound like a prophesy: "Multilateralism is something that we Europeans believe in and for which we Europeans have provided a blueprint. It's a key element for ensuring a secure future for the world we live in. And we must be the shining example. If we bungle the European Union – and we're on the way to doing that when we blame Europe for everything that goes wrong – we will not get the strong leadership we need from the European Union in any of its institutions or manifestations. And if we bungle it, history will judge our failure harshly, since we

make fundamental, lasting and immediate changes. It can't be about selfishness or interests; it has to be about the way we see the world and the way we see ourselves."

One guest summed it up powerfully back then: "Would you board an airplane that had a five percent chance of crashing? Of course not. But the world is in much greater danger." Accordingly, the Millennium Development Goals, climate change and renewable energies were also discussed. The participants agreed that humanity faces a multitude of interrelated, urgent and global challenges that can only be overcome through global cooperation and long-term strategies.

The practical recommendations from 15 years ago are still highly relevant:

- Dialogue must be fostered and expanded in different world regions and on different levels.
- Partnerships, alliances and networks must be created across different sectors and levels, and they must include art, business and politics so they can learn from each other and make effective use of existing knowledge, technology and resources.
- The potential women have to offer must be activated. Their voices must be heard in this dialogue on all levels – from local communities to the United Nations – and on all issues. Not only what is said is important, but also who says it.
- Respected global thinkers should be given a platform to share and develop their ideas. For certain topics, expert groups can help by producing detailed analysis and action plans based on that analysis.
- Global learning requires a serious evaluation of teaching curricula from around the world, which must include elements that promote global thinking and global citizenship.
- Existing international institutions must be strengthened and coordinated more effectively. It must also be clarified which other types of international institutions need to be created.
- An open-source platform for generating and disseminating ideas must be established to promote public discourse. In addition to global activities, action must be taken in key areas on the local

level. To make use of the remaining window of opportunity and respond adequately to global challenges, it will be necessary, among other things, to reduce the consumption of natural resources, fulfill international agreements (Millennium Development Goals, aid for Africa, the Kyoto Protocol, etc.), identify common values and create effective global institutions – goals that were well out of reach in 2008 and that remain so today.

Thoughts on Social Values and Social Cohesion

Edda Moser
Opera Singer and University Instructor

If we are talking about global responsibility, what is Europe's message (or what should it be)?

> *In my opinion, this means paying tribute to the now, while never forgetting the past, but always taking it as a warning and responsibility, since that is what prevents harm and safeguards progress – and helpfully bringing confidence, diligence, the latest knowledge and the European-global message to the peoples, while remaining humbly cognizant of this planet's uniqueness.*

Democracy is based on the effort to achieve a consensus between majorities and minorities. Is this basis still intact and functional?

> *Democracy will always require effort to endure people who think differently, since my perspective can seem unreasonable to those with attitudes diametrically opposed to mine, and since democracy has a lot to do with tolerating political views that are foreign to me and can thus be hard to sustain.*

What is our vision today of a liberal democracy? Which arguments can we deploy to convince people of its necessity and its benefits?

> *Given our conception of freedom ("freedom is the freedom of the other"), our vision of a generally liberal democracy will never approach*

Photo Credits

Marion Custred/Alpensektor: cover, pp. 89–93, 94 top
Jürgen Dannenberg/Alpensektor: pp. 76 bottom, 77–88, 94 bottom, 95, 96
Christoph Gödan: pp. 71 bottom, 72
Bernhard J. Holzner/Hopi-Media: pp. 66–70, 71 top, 73, 74, 75 top
Private source: inside flap, p. 9 (Wolfgang Schüssel)
Dr. Wolfgang Schüssel: drawing pp. 40/41
Jan Voth: inside flap, p. 9 (Liz Mohn)
Arne Weychardt: pp. 75 top, 76 bottom

The titles in the captions refer to positions held at the time the
photographs were taken.

the ideal, since the joy of a disciplined upbringing, education, religion, custom, past, literature, art, vision of other peoples will give rise in very different ways to variously justified misunderstandings...

20 years of the Trilogue Salzburg: What was your "Trilogue moment"?

My personal Trilogue moment: my first encounter with Mrs. Liz Mohn, since our attitude toward "happiness" turned out to be wonderfully the same.